GLOUCESTERSHIRE
PAST

A GUIDE TO HISTORIC PLACES AND PEOPLE

ANN MOORE

ALAN SUTTON PUBLISHING LIMITED

First published in the United Kingdom in 1995
Alan Sutton Publishing Ltd · Phoenix Mill · Far Thrupp · Stroud · Gloucestershire

British Library Cataloguing in Publication Data

A catalogue record for this book is available from the British Library

ISBN 0-7509-0945-5

Typeset in 9/13 Sabon.
Typesetting and origination by
Alan Sutton Publishing Limited.
Printed in Great Britain by
Ebenezer Baylis, Worcester.

CONTENTS

INTRODUCTION		vii
MAP		viii
AMPNEY CRUCIS	*A Church Where Time is Important*	1
ASHCHURCH	*A Public Punishment*	2
ASHLEWORTH	*A Past Barn in Present Use*	3
	A Ferry Boat Inn	4
AVENING	*Man With a Secret Past*	5
BERKELEY	*'Right Famous as the Seat of Barons Bold'*	6
	To Improve the View	7
	The Last Jester	8
	A Man Who Ran Out of Time	9
BIBURY	*Perpetual Crystal Waters*	10
BISLEY	*'A Well of Living Waters'*	11
	To Pray for Poor Souls	12
BOURTON-ON- THE-WATER	*Everything in Miniature*	13
	Caught in the Trap!	14
BROADWAY	*A Guide for Every Coachman*	15
BROOKTHORPE	*A Unique Chronogram*	16
CHALFORD	*Round We Go!*	17
CHELTENHAM	*Bubbles of Time*	18
	A Man With Job Satisfaction	19
CHIPPING CAMPDEN	*A Treasured Market Hall*	20
	No Surrender	21
	'A Marchant ther was . . .'	22
CHURCHDOWN	*High on a Hill*	23
CIRENCESTER	*The First Word Square?*	24
	A Sham Castle and Grand Vistas	25
	A Poet's Bower	26
	The Largest Parish Church in *Gloucestershire*	27
CLEARWELL	*A Light from Nelly*	28
	A 'Labyrinth of Mining History'	29
COBERLY	*A Heart Burial*	30
DAGLINGWORTH	*A Medieval Dovecote*	31
DEERHURST	*A Saxon Priory Church*	32
	Her Faithful Friend	33
	For My Brother Elfric	34
DIDMARTON	*A Triple-decker Pulpit*	35
	Hat Pegs for Giants?	36

DOVER'S HILL	The Cotswold Olympicks	37
	An Original 'Moot' Point	38
DUMBLETON	A Primitive Green Man	39
DYMOCK	Where Daffodils Run 'in Golden Tides'	40
	The Old Cottage	41
	The Dymock Curse	42
ELKSTONE	A Priest's Dovecote	43
EPNEY	A Surfeit of . . . Eels	44
FAIRFORD	Come, See My Scriptures in Glass	45
	Pictures of the Past and a Treacle Bible	46
FARMINGTON	A Horse-lover's Gate	47
FLAXLEY	St Anthony's Well	48
FOREST OF DEAN	The Speech House	49
FORTHAMPTON	Unnecessary Stocks?	50
GLOUCESTER	The First War Memorial	51
	The Monks at Play	52
	Bishop Hooper's House	53
	Centuries of Welcome	54
	Where Once Were Bells	55
	British (Isles) Time	56
GREAT BARRINGTON	Never to Draw Sword Again	57
	For a Fisherman	58
GUITING POWER	Maintaining the Breeds	59
HAILES ABBEY	'The blood of Crist that is in Hales'	60
HARTPURY	An Ancient Home for Bees	61
KEMPLEY	Frescoes for a Father	62
LECHLADE	Old Father Thames	63
LITTLEDEAN	A Deliberate Mistake?	64
	House With a Past	65
LOWER SLAUGHTER	The Village Mill	66
	Cotswold Home for One Thousand	67
LOWER SWELL	A Striking Bell Turret	68
MAISEMORE	Bridge With a History	69
MORETON IN MARSH	A Toll Board	70
NEWENT	Victorian Newent	71
	A Tomb With a Mystery	72
	'Wine that Maketh Glad the Heart'	73
NEWLAND	Cathedral of the Forest	74
	A Freeminer of Dean	75
NEWNHAM ON SEVERN	The Legend of the Grasshopper and the Ant	76
	Today It Must Be Wednesday	77
NORTH CERNEY	For Ease of Entry	78
	To See a Manticore	79
NORTHLEACH	A Famous Family Brass	80
NORTH NIBLEY	In Memory of Tyndale	81

PAINSWICK	*Spectacle Stocks*	82
	Remember Drake	83
PRESTBURY	*Home of a Famous Jockey*	84
RODBOROUGH	*Home Is a Folly*	85
RUDDLE	*A Forgotten Port*	86
RUDFORD	*In Memory of a Massacre*	87
RYEFORD	*Defying Any Fire*	88
ST BRIAVELS	*An Ancient Bread and Cheese Ceremony*	89
SAPPERTON	*'Legging It'*	90
SHAPRIDGE	*Charcoal Furnace and Mill*	91
SHARPNESS	*The First Commercial Nuclear Power Station*	92
SNOWSHILL	*A Treasure Trove*	93
	An Astrological Clock	94
SOUTHAM	*Grain Distribution Point*	95
STANWAY	*A Cotswold Pyramid*	96
	An Ice House	97
STAUNTON	*Ancient Standing Stones*	98
STOW-ON-THE-WOLD	*Corn Returns*	99
	More 'Wool' Tombs	100
SUDELEY	*A Noble Castle and Home*	101
	'A Court for Owls'	102
SYDE	*Syde's 'Hidden Gem'*	103
TEDDINGTON	*'Strange Travellers the Way to Show'*	104
TETBURY	*A Wool Centre*	105
	An Early Gothic Revival Church	106
	Our Own Beer	107
TEWKESBURY	*Truly Belonging to the People*	108
	Home of the Baptist Faith	109
TREDINGTON	*Back to the Jurassic Age*	110
ULEY	*Hetty Peglar's Tump*	111
WESTBURY ON SEVERN	*The Watch Tower*	112
WINCHCOMBE	*Seven Legs?*	113
	Find the Imp	114
	Safely Locked Away	115
	Treasures for the Steam Enthusiast	116
	Trainee Sign Writer?	117
WYCK RISSINGTON	*A Mosaic Maze*	118
ACKNOWLEDGEMENTS		119
BIBLIOGRAPHY		120

The roundhouse at Chalford

INTRODUCTION

Look at a map and Gloucestershire is just like any other county, but explore it, and you will find that it is as rich and diverse as any in the British Isles. It sprawls across two Ordnance Survey maps and reaches into four others, and within its 1,030 square miles lie busy towns and timeless rural villages, deep forest, river valleys and the famous Cotswolds. Each area holds on to its particular history, each area is different, but it is still part of Gloucestershire. The county's name first appeared in written records about 1016, and derives from the city's Celtic name 'Caer Glow', 'the beautiful city'. Like other counties, Gloucestershire was victim to the presumptuous Local Government Act of 1972 when old county lines were re-drawn, and it lost part of its southern area to the new Avon; but the natural divisions of Forest, Vale and Hills were left untouched, and books about Gloucestershire often specialize in these areas. In this book, however, the county is taken as a whole, and because of this, I may only give a flavour of all that can be found within its boundaries.

This is a personal and by no means definitive collection of things which I have found interesting or unusual. Some are hidden away, others are obvious and some widely advertised on the 'tourist trail' are not here at all; but they are all things which have led me to wonder or to ask 'Why?' Historical, religious or everyday things of the past – I have found them interesting enough to want to find out more about them and record them. In some cases these objects may soon be swept away, in others they will continue to stand proudly as part of Gloucestershire's heritage, the past upon which every 'present' is built. I hope you will enjoy my collection and, where applicable, do your part in preserving these places for others to find. If I have done nothing else in preparing this book, I have come to appreciate and enjoy the beautiful, and to me new, county of Gloucestershire in all its diversity, and I look forward to visiting it again and again.

Ann Moore

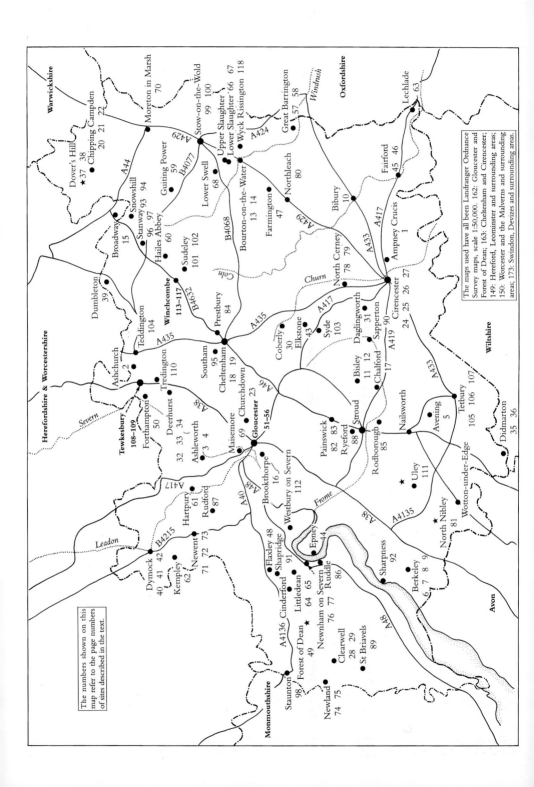

Warwickshire

Oxfordshire

Dover's Hill
★ 37 38
Chipping Campden
20 21 22

Moreton in Marsh
70

Windrush

Lechlade
63

A44

Stow-on-the-Wold
99 100

Guiting Power
59

Upper Slaughter 66 67
Lower Slaughter 66
Wyck Rissington 118

Great Barrington
57 58

Snowshill 94
Stanway 93 94

B4077

A424

Fairford
45 46

Broadway
15

Hailes Abbey
60

Lower Swell
68

Bourton-on-the-Water
13 14

Northleach
80

Bibury
10

Ampney Crucis
1

Dumbleton
39

Sudeley
101 102

B4632

Farmington
47

A433

A417

B4068

Coln

Winchcombe
113–117

Prestbury
84

Churn

North Cerney
78 79

Cirencester
24 25 26 27

Teddington
104

A435

A417

Coberly
30

Syde
103

Daglingworth
31

A419

A433

Tetbury
105 106 107

Ashchurch
2

Southam
95

Cheltenham
18 19

Elkstone
43

Sapperton

Bisley
11 12

Chalford
17

Tredington
110

Churchdown
23

Didmarton
35 36

Severn

Tewkesbury
108–109

Deerhurst
34

Maisemore
69

Gloucester
51–56

Painswick
82 83

Rodborough
85

Stroud

Nailsworth

Avening
5

Forthampton
50

Ashleworth
32 33 34
3 4

A38

Ryeford
88

Uley
111

A417

Brookthorpe

Westbury on Severn
112

Frome

A4135

North Nibley
81

Wotton-under-Edge

Leadon

Hartpury
61

Rudford
87

A40

A48

Epney
44

Wick on Severn
86

Sharpness
92

Berkeley
6 7 8 9

B4215

Dymock
40 41 42

Kempley
62

Newent
71 72 73

Flaxley 48
Shapridge
91

Littledean
64 65

Ruddle
86

A38

A48

Avon

A4136 Cinderford

Newnham on Severn
76 77

Clearwell
28 29

St Briavels
89

Staunton
98

Forest of Dean
49

Newland
74 75

Monmouthshire

Wiltshire

Herefordshire & Worcestershire

The numbers shown on this
map refer to the page numbers
of sites described in the text.

The maps used have all been Landranger Ordnance
Survey maps, scale 1:50,000. 162: Gloucester and
Forest of Dean; 163: Cheltenham and Cirencester;
149: Hereford, Leominster and surrounding areas;
150: Worcester and the Malverns and surrounding
areas; 173: Swindon, Devizes and surrounding areas.

AMPNEY CRUCIS

A Church Where Time is Important

Location: 3 miles
east of Cirencester
off A417, ¼ mile
down a side road

MAP REFERENCE:
163: 065019

It is unusual to find a memorial where the actual time of death is recorded, but here in this dedication we learn that Robert Pleydall, Squire, died on 4 January in the year 1675, 'between the hours of 2 and 3 am, having lived for almost 58 years'. It would seem from the inscription that Squire Pleydall, a second son, was a pious, modest and temperate man, and one who was 'friendly to strangers', although why this phrase should have been written in Greek is a mystery. Perhaps the word had some significance for the family, or perhaps the writer wished to show he was conversant with the language. This is one of four tablets set in the east wall of the transept. Nearby on the pulpit stands an hourglass, its metal stand in the wall beside it. No longer used, its trickling sands were doubtless much valued by parishioners enduring a wearying sermon.

OTHER PLACES
OF INTEREST

*Cirencester to the
west (p. 24);
Barnsley House
garden to the north;
Fairford to the east
(p. 45).*

ASHCHURCH

A Public Punishment

The stocks here at Ashchurch are placed in such a position that anyone being forced into them would suffer the maximum humiliation. They stand beside the gate at the foot of the path leading to St Nicholas' church, so that those attending service – and that would be the majority of the village population when these stocks were used – would have to pass the wrongdoer; a sure way, one would think, of inflicting mental as well as physical punishment. The guilty would have to reflect on their sins before the eyes of all their world. The church itself is generally kept locked now.

OTHER PLACES OF INTEREST

Tewkesbury to the west (p. 108); Deerhurst and Tredington to the south (pp. 32, 110).

ASHLEWORTH

A Past Barn in Present Use

This tithe barn, scheduled as an ancient monument and under the protection of the National Trust, may be over 500 years old, but it is still a working barn. Today its Cotswold stone roof shelters hay, straw and other things common through the centuries as well as modern items such as a tractor. Built between 1481 and 1515 by Abbot Newberry, it is 125 ft long and 25 ft wide with two bays and very narrow slit windows. The court adjacent to the barn is said to have belonged to Gloucester's Black Friars. The house as it stands was built around 1460 and is little changed, apart from minor alterations and a slate rather than a thatched roof.

The church, dedicated to St Andrew, was built slightly later, although a church here had been granted to the Abbey of St Augustine at Bristol in 1154.

ASHLEWORTH

A Ferry Boat Inn

Beyond the tithe barn, a walk, pleasant in summer but decidedly muddy in winter, takes one to the west bank of the Severn and the old quay. There has been a ferry here for a long time, and in former days the Boat Inn which marks its landing point would have seen more custom than it does now. The house, which has been extended over the

years, belonged to the Jelf family whose ancestors, it is said, ferried Charles I across the river. In recognition of this act, the grateful monarch granted them a charter, giving them the monopoly of the ferry for ever. The neat little building at the front, with its rounded wall, was once a brewhouse, for the family, in common with most people centuries ago, brewed their own ale.

OTHER PLACES
OF INTEREST

Hartpury to the
south-west (p. 61);
Maisemore to the
south (p. 69);
Gloucester to the
south-east (p. 51).

AVENING

Man With a Secret Past

Location: 2½ miles
south-east of
Nailsworth on
B4014

MAP REFERENCE:
162: 880980

One might not expect this impressive-looking figure, son of a Tudor lord, to have had anything more exciting in his life than the obligatory field of battle, the odd clandestine affair or tales of gambling and card playing. But if history is to be believed, Henry Bridges led a fascinating, if unworthy, life before he settled down. In the days of his youth, it is said, he was a notorious highwayman, a smuggler and a pirate. Then he met and married the daughter of a clothier, a rich and important trade at the end of the sixteenth century, and became a reformed character. His autobiography would have made interesting reading.

OTHER PLACES
OF INTEREST

Nailsworth to the
north; Tetbury to
the south (p. 105).

Location: 2 miles along the B4066, off A38, 19 miles south-west of Gloucester

MAP REFERENCE:
162: 686990

BERKELEY

'*Right Famous as the Seat of Barons Bold*'

Michael Drayton

No-one could write about Gloucestershire's past without including Berkeley Castle, a building so full of history and yet so accessible to us today. Built as a fortress 800 years ago, added to and lived in continuously by the Berkeley family ever since, it is not only part of Gloucestershire's past but of Great Britain's too, and yet, although 'savage' and old, it has gradually been transformed into a castle home. Guides and an excellent booklet take the visitor through this history, but it is the detail which is interesting – sixteenth-century embroidered wallpaper on the grand stairs, solid lead sinks in the buttery, the beautiful Tudor spider-web ceiling in the kitchen and the unusual and imaginative ring handle on the outside of the buttery door – not a surfeit of lampreys perhaps, but definitely two.

BERKELEY

To *Improve the View*

A s she sat sewing beside a window in the small drawing-room, Elizabeth Drax, wife of the 4th Earl Berkeley (1716–55), often looked out across the grounds, but she did not like what she saw. The gardens were neat, the meadowlands beyond pleasant, but in the distance the Hunt kennels met with her disfavour – they were a blot on her landscape.

So, to please her, this handsome façade, an 'eyecatcher', was built across from the kennels. The buildings it hid were headquarters of the oldest Hunt in England, founded in 1067 by Roger de Berkeley, whose land for the next 750 years stretched from the Severn to London. After a split in the early 1800s, the Berkeley Hunt still covered an area of some 350 miles. Elizabeth, meanwhile, continued contentedly with her embroidery, and some of her amazing work forms the covering for a suite of gilt furniture in the long drawing-room – meticulous fine petit-point in still glowing rich colours.

BERKELEY

The Last Jester

This is one of several notable tombs in the churchyard of the Church of St Mary the Virgin adjacent to the castle. The Norman church, with its separate eighteenth-century tower, has much of interest inside, including an alabaster tomb to the Lord Berkeley who was responsible for the castle's beautiful great hall and who was accused of complicity in the murder of Edward II.

But this tomb lies to the left of the path approaching the church. It is the resting place of Dickie Pearce, said to be the last jester in England, who, in 1728, aged sixty-three, fell from the gallery in the aforementioned great hall and died a few days later. His full epitaph, written by Dean Swift, begs one not to mourn the fool's passing too much, since 'Dickys enough are still behind' for us to laugh at.

BERKELEY

A Man Who Ran Out of Time

Near the same church door is another well-known memorial, coincidentally to a man whose name is only different in its spelling – Thomas Pierce. He died at the age of seventy-seven, on 25 February 1665. He was a watchmaker skilled in making 'Jacks and Clocks and Watches' in 'Iron, Brasse and Silver', but a man who 'when his own watch was down to the last . . . had not Key to winde it up'.

Thomas, however, was a much respected man, having been mayor five times during his life. Doubtless he was as much missed as a citizen as he was as a watchmaker.

OTHER PLACES OF INTEREST

Nibley to the north-west (p. 81); Sharpness to the north (p. 92); Slimbridge to the north-east.

BIBURY

Location: 7 miles
north-east of
Cirencester on the
B4425 to Burford
MAP REFERENCE:
163: 116069

Perpetual Crystal Waters

This sparkling spring gushing beneath overhanging willows by the river Cohn can be seen from the road, but it is best viewed from neat private water gardens nearby. These belong to the adjacent Swan Hotel, an old coaching inn and still an attractive Cotswold building clad in scarlet creepers in·autumn. It is said that the spring gushes 2½ million gallons of water every twenty-four hours, and it is as clear as water could possibly be.

Nearby is the Bibury trout farm, one of the first in England, where rainbow trout are bred and reared in twenty ponds and where visitors are welcome daily. Just across the river is Arlington, with its row of pretty seventeenth-century cottages (now owned by the National Trust) and an old corn mill on the A433, also from the seventeenth century, and now housing the Cotswold Country Museum.

OTHER PLACES
OF INTEREST

Barnsley House
gardens to the
south-west;
Northleach to the
north (p. 80);
Burford (Oxon)
Cotswold Wildlife
Park to the east.

BISLEY

'A Well of Living Waters'

For generations the people of Bisley took advantage of the waters which tumbled from natural springs in the heart of the village. Then in 1863 this well-head, with its seven spouts, was restored by Thomas Keble, vicar here from 1827 to 1873, complete with the exhortation: 'Ye Wells, Bless ye the Lord, Praise Him, and Magnify Him for ever'. By tradition each Ascension Day, after a special service, a procession descends from the church above to decorate the well-head with flowers.

Beside the well fifty-one steps, restored in 1896, lead the way back into the rear grounds of the church, one step halfway up advising the climber to 'Seek those things which are above'.

Another unusual building nearby is the village lock-up in George Street. This 'blind house', with its ogee gable, was built in 1824 to replace a former one which adjoined the churchyard, and consists of two cells, one for women and one for men.

BISLEY

To Pray for Poor Souls

Bisley church may be reached by the well-head steps or by a rise from the main street. Here one finds this unique Poor Souls' Light, the only external one in England. Six-sided and with a central covered 'bone hole', it is a chantry where candles were lit for the souls of the poor.

Legend says it was built in the thirteenth century, over a well into which, one dark and stormy night, a parish priest fell and was drowned. The monument was ordered by some high authority, perhaps even the Pope, who also decreed that as punishment for the negligence in leaving the well uncovered, parishioners could arrange no burials at Bisley for two years. Instead, they had to arrange for them to be held at Bibury, some 15 miles away. There may be some truth in this, for a section of Bibury's churchyard was known as 'the Bisley piece' and the long cross-country path between the churches as Dead Man's Lane. Bisley church was founded in the eleventh century and extensively restored in the mid-1800s.

OTHER PLACES OF INTEREST

Chalford to the south (p. 17); Cirencester Park to the south-east (p. 25); Misarden Park gardens to the north-east.

BOURTON-ON-THE-WATER

Everything in Miniature

*Location: 4 miles
south-west of Stow-
on-the-Wold, off
A429*

MAP REFERENCE:
163: 170206

These strange stunted little figures are there to welcome visitors to a famous tourist venue. Long established, Bourton's model village was opened on Coronation Day in 1937 here in the garden behind the Old New Inn by its landlord, Mr Morris (the original inn dated back to 1712). One-ninth of the size of Bourton, the model is extremely accurate and detailed. It took eight men four years, using old local Cotswold stone, to recreate the village as it then was and it is complete, even down to a model of the model.

The village itself, once referred to as 'the little Venice of the Cotswolds', is very pretty, its main street meandering beside the Windrush. The clear water and the little low bridges invite one to linger, although it is doubtful whether the Roman Legion that crossed one of them was allowed to do so.

BOURTON-ON-THE-WATER

Caught in the Trap!

The Mousetrap is unique in being the only inn in England to bear this name, and its fame has spread so far that it is even featured in the programme of the longest-running play of the same name in London! But it hasn't always been The Mousetrap. Before the early 1980s, it was the Landsdowne Inn, and it had been for well over a hundred years.

Its 'new' name relates to an incident some years earlier when, it is said, Irish navvies were working in the area. Unable to afford meat, their lunches generally consisted of bread and cheese. Now these navvies, the story goes, were work-shy, and one day disappeared into a small back room here in the inn for a snack. Their foreman came in and caught them, not working, but eating their cheese like mice in a trap! And The Mousetrap this inn has been ever since.

*OTHER PLACES
OF INTEREST*

*Folly Farm to the
west; the Slaughters
and Stow to the
north (pp. 66, 99);
Northleach to the
south (p. 80).*

BROADWAY

A Guide for Every Coachman

Location: at the junction of the A44 Evesham to Oxford and B4081 Chipping Campden to Stanway roads

MAP REFERENCE:
151: 135390

Anyone rushing along in a modern car could be forgiven for missing this signpost, for its fingers point direction and mileage about 10 ft above the road. Tall and slim, it is about ¼ mile from the top of the steep Fish Hill and is half-hidden by a large spreading beech tree. Standing on the site of an old gallows, it would have been at the correct height for coach travellers, pointing the way to 'Oxford XXIIII miles, The way to Gloster XVIII miles NI, The way to Warwick XV miles, The way to Woster XVI miles NI' (sic), all the mileages being those recorded on the post in 1669.

OTHER PLACES OF INTEREST

Snowshill, 2 miles south of Broadway (p. 93).

BROOKTHORPE

A Unique Chronogram

Here in the wall of St Swithin's church porch is a solid beam which is unique. Incised along its length is a chronogram – a sentence in which is hidden a date. In a single line the words read:

RW Ter Deno IanI Labens reX soLe Ca Dente CaroLVs eXVtVs soLIo sCeptroqVe se CVre.

Translated, this reads: RW Dying on 30 January, unconcernedly at sunset, King Charles having been stripped of his throne and authority.

The chronogram is found in the capital letters which are incorporated and which add up to 1648 when Charles I was clearly defeated. He was executed on 30 January 1649.

These are the roman numerals:

2 Ds	=	1,000
4 Cs	=	400
4 Ls	=	200
2 Xs	=	20
5 Vs	=	25
3 Is	=	3
		1648

The initials RW are thought to represent Roland Wood, lord of the manor here and a Royalist supporter: that he should 'die unconcernedly at sunset' shows the depths of his despair. One can only wonder at Wood's loyalty and the ingenuity in the chronogram, and hope that the beam is respected and allowed to carry its message to those who understand it for many centuries to come.

OTHER PLACES
OF INTEREST

Painswick to the
south-east (p. 82).

CHALFORD

Round We Go!

This unusual roundhouse formed part of the network of the Thames Severn Canal in the eighteenth and nineteenth centuries (see p. 90). Situated at the foot of a hill in the Golden Valley, and below the church, it was built in 1790 for a canal worker. It was his responsibility to act as watchman and to see that this particular area of the canal and its environs was well maintained. Living here must have been akin to living in a lighthouse, although the narrow windows must have made for dark rooms when candles and lamps were the source of light. The cramped conditions could not have been easy for any man with a large family. The building is well preserved and still used, not as a home, but as a studio for craftsmen.

OTHER PLACES OF INTEREST

Cirencester and its park to the east (p. 24); Bisley to the north (p. 11).

*Location: 6 miles
from Gloucester
along A40*
Map reference:
163: 950223

CHELTENHAM

Bubbles of Time

The now famous Wishing Fish Clock in the Regent Arcade is almost as great an attraction as Cheltenham's architecture, shops and parks. Created by Kit Williams, famous for his book *Masquerade*, it was unveiled in January 1987, having been twelve months in the making. From the large white duck at its top to the great 12 ft wooden fish beneath the clock, the whole mechanism, weighing over 3 tons and stretching more than 45 ft, is said to be the longest in the world. The structural and working parts of the clock were built by the respected clockmaker Michael Harding at a cost of £80,000. Set against a blue-starred background, the clock is enchanting. Around its face various doors pop open, seemingly at random, to reveal mice and a snake,

while the sun revolves to indicate the hours and the duck, over 50 ft above the shopping mall, lays a continual stream of golden eggs. The *pièce de résistance*, however, occurs every half hour. Then the fish rolls its eyes, shakes its tail and, to the tune of 'I'm forever blowing bubbles', blows a stream of bubbles into the mall – catch one, and you may make a wish!

CHELTENHAM

A Man With Job Satisfaction

Location: St Mary's
churchyard

MAP REFERENCE:
163: 948226

Although Cheltenham is known as a distinguished area, a spa town, it has always been home to 'ordinary' people, and none more ordinary than John Higgs, pig killer, who died on 26 November 1826, aged fifty-four years. His grave, worn away by time and the weather, lies beside the path to the east of St Mary's church door. Some words, assumed here in brackets, have flaked away, but this appears to be the epitaph of an industrious man who clearly enjoyed his work and had no sons to follow in his footsteps.

Here lies John Higgs
A famous man for killing pigs.
Killing pigs was his delight
(Both) morning, afternoon and night.
(Both h)eats and cold h(e did) endure.
When no physician could (him) cure
His knife is laid, his work is done
I hope to heaven his soul is gone.

All four sons of the above
had died in their infancy.

OTHER PLACES
OF INTEREST

Elkstone to the
south (p. 43);
Chedworth Roman
Villa to the south-
east.

CHIPPING CAMPDEN

A Treasured Market Hall

The Market Hall has stood here for more than 360 years and is so well cared for by the National Trust that it should stand for many centuries to come. It was built in 1627 by Sir Baptist Hicks (see p. 21), and under its fine stone arches stall-holders gathered to sell butter, cheese and poultry.

Other ancient golden stone buildings line the High Street of this once rich and important wool town. Medieval monastic doorways, gabled houses and the lovely fourteenth-century house of wool merchant William Grevel (see p. 22), with its two-storeyed bay window, transport the visitor back through the centuries, to a time which to us may seem unhurried and peaceful, but which was probably just as fraught with its own problems as are our modern times.

CHIPPING CAMPDEN

No Surrender

Beside the imposing Church of St James, with its elegant pinnacled 120 ft tower, stands this equally impressive, although restored, gateway to what was once Campden House. It was built by wealthy silk merchant Sir Baptist Hicks (d. 1629), who also built the graceful almshouses in Church Street in the 1620s. For a while Campden House was his home, and the ruins give some indication of how magnificent it must have been.

Sir Baptist was a philanthropist and a great friend of Charles I, and as a Royalist, during the Civil War, he had his lovely home burned to the ground rather than allow it to fall into the hands of the Parliamentarians. Sir Baptist, one of the church's benefactors, is buried in the Gainsborough Chapel to the right of the chancel, with his wife and other members of the family. There are ornate sculptures standing to his memory.

CHIPPING CAMPDEN

'A Marchant ther was . . .'

Chaucer, *Canterbury Tales*, Prologue, l. 270

St James' Church is also the resting place of another of its benefactors, a man who lived two centuries before Sir Baptist Hicks. William Grevel, who died on 1 October 1401, left 100 marks to be used for 'the new work' in the church's rebuilding – probably the north aisle and the north chapel where he lies. His great memorial brass, at 8 ft 9 in x 4 ft 4 in, said to be the largest in the country, is now in front of the communion rails. It is just possible to see that like Chaucer's Merchant he had the short hair, moustache and 'a forked berd' which only elders wore. He is noted as being 'The flower of wool merchants of all England'.

Other items of interest in the church include a medieval cope, the only perfect set of fifteenth-century altar hangings in England and monuments including one to Sir Thomas Smith, a courtier to Henry VII.

OTHER PLACES OF INTEREST

Dover's Hill to the north-west (p. 37); Kiftsgate Court gardens to the north; Hidcote Manor Garden to the north-east.

CHURCHDOWN

High on a Hill

The old church of St Bartholomew stands high above the village on Chosen Hill, and before the narrow winding metal road was built it could be reached only by a path up which, in wintry weather, coffins were dragged by sled. It stands on an ancient, partly man-made mound which may pre-date the Iron Age, and limited excavations are currently revealing evidence of an earlier building and graveyard here. The upper storey of the porch, now closed, shows the windows of a tiny room complete with fireplace. The chimney has gone, but the room must have been a welcome refuge for priests from Gloucester who stayed here when on a visit. These visitors must needs have been very slim, for the room is reached via steps through an extremely narrow arched doorway

inside the church. The porch also reveals ancient graffiti scratched on its walls, faint now after centuries of weather; and inside the bell tower, several inches from the floor, another unknown artist hundreds of years ago painted a small green windmill – why, no-one knows.

OTHER PLACES
OF INTEREST

Cheltenham to the
east (p. 18).

CIRENCESTER

The First Word Square?

Thousands of years ago someone, probably a Roman, scratched an acrostic on plaster, and this unique example of an early word puzzle was found here in Gloucestershire. Discovered in 1868 during excavations in a garden in what is now Victoria Road, its origin and meaning have given rise to much debate, especially since only two others like it have ever been found, and they in Pompeii. It is thought that although the words are repeated in different directions (meaning literally 'The Sower Arepo holds the wheels with force'), the square could be an anagram of PATERNOSTER and the letters A and O repeated twice. This would represent the first two words of the Lord's Prayer with the Alpha and Omega, referring to Christ as the beginning and the end, repeated twice. Before this discovery, acrostics were thought to be medieval in origin and generally used as a charm or talisman. Since this square probably dates back to the first century AD, the secrets of its existence, and whether or not it was a Christian symbol, will provide debate for scholars for years to come.

Other fascinating views of Roman life may also be found in the Corinium Museum.

CIRENCESTER

A Sham Castle and Grand Vistas

The Romans may have left literary puzzles and straight roads in Cirencester, but others in succeeding centuries have made their mark too. Cirencester Park, 3,000 acres of beautiful parkland, was created in the early eighteenth century by the remarkable 1st Earl, Lord Bathurst, who left a legacy of geometric landscaping with avenues, rides and follies which, thanks to his successors' generosity, we may still enjoy today. Alfred's Hall, built in 1721, is surrounded by dark firs and evergreens. With its tower and irregular castellated walls and its truly medieval appearance, it has been described by the writer Barbara Jones as being 'a building which it is difficult to equal as a convincing sham'. It is one of eight folly buildings and was designed by the earl with his friend Alexander Pope the poet. To see these follies one must be prepared to walk some distance, for the park is for walkers only, although during the summer polo matches are often held here at weekends.

CIRENCESTER

A Poet's Bower

The 1st Earl of Bathurst was referred to several times in the work of the eighteenth-century poet Alexander Pope (1688–1744), and Pope often came to Cirencester as the earl's guest. It was during one of these visits between 1715 and 1725 that they designed Alfred's Hall (see previous page), and much of the parkland itself. Many of the trees were planted by Pope and in his 'Third Moral Essay on the Use of Riches' he refers to 'these sacred shades . . . the finest wood in England'. Here, at the crest of a rise along a path at the eastern end of the park, he designed and had built this seat – a 'bower' where he, a 'hermit of Twickenham', might rest and possibly think out the satirical verse for which he is famous.

CIRENCESTER

The Largest Parish Church in Gloucestershire

Perhaps the most commanding building in Cirencester, and possibly the most photographed, is the solid Church of St John the Baptist in the Market Square, with its Perpendicular tower and its two-storeyed porch. Both the 162 ft tower and the porch were begun in about 1400, and for a long time the porch's upper storey was used as a town hall. Visitors will find much of interest within the church – there is too much to mention here. It also boasts the oldest peal of twelve bells in the country and customs to go with them. On 29 May bells are still rung at 6 a.m. to mark the restoration of the Monarchy, and the Pancake Bell rings out on Shrove Tuesday.

In the quiet and often ignored churchyard behind the church lie the usual memorials, including one to Sarah Avery who bid the world adieu in 1833 at the age of eighty. For thirty-seven years she had been a midwife, helping women:

> . . . in nature's trying hour
> Through heat and cold by day and dreary night
> To save the hapless was my soul's delight.

OTHER PLACES
OF INTEREST

Cirencester Brewery
Arts Workshop,
Brewery Court;
Chedworth Roman
Villa to the north.

Location: 1½ miles
south of Coleford
on B4228
MAP REFERENCE:
162: 575083

CLEARWELL

A Light from Nelly

Before carbide lamps came into use in the 1880s, a 'nelly' like this was a freeminer's constant companion as he worked more than 500 ft below ground in the ancient iron ore mines of Clearwell in the Forest of Dean. 'Nelly' was the name given to the ball of clay into which, at the top, was stuck a candle. Then a forked stick about 6 in long was

pushed into the side of the nelly. This stick was held between the teeth, across the mouth, the candle at the side, so that the miner had light but also had both hands free for working. Each candle lasted one hour so, since a working shift lasted ten hours, the miner knew how far into his shift he was; but to avoid being plunged into darkness, he also had a 'nest' of nellies nearby. A simple and ingenious idea, but not one many of us would care to use today.

CLEARWELL

A 'Labyrinth of Mining History'

Iron ore has been mined beneath the Royal Forest of Dean for over 2,500 years and the result is a maze of underground caverns, or 'churns', and tunnels. The last iron ore raised here commercially was in 1945, and now eight of the caverns are open to the public. The one illustrated is the Frozen Waterfall Chamber. It is named after the fine calcite flow, which resembles a waterfall in winter. Calcite is normally white, but if the picture were in colour, you would see that here it is coloured by iron oxides to an orange-pink shade.

Centuries ago, using one-bladed pickaxes and wooden shovels, freeminers piled the ore into 'billies', wood and leather containers strapped to a boy's back, and these were pulled to the surface. It was not until the Act of 1842 that women and children ceased to labour below ground. Between 1832 and 1880, 524,299 tons of iron ore were extracted from these mines.

Excellent books and guides give much information, and tours and caving trips are available. Open every day March–October.

OTHER PLACES
OF INTEREST

Coleford to the
north; Newland to
the north-west
(p. 74); St Briavels
to the south (p. 89).

COBERLY

*Location: 2 miles
south of
Cheltenham, off
A435 beyond its
junction with A436,
and through the
private grounds of
Coberly Hall*
MAP REFERENCE:
163: 966158

A Heart Burial

Crusading knights often willed that upon death their hearts should return home for burial even if it were not possible for their bodies to do so. This desire remained with Sir Giles Berkeley. A crusader in his youth, he did not die in battle, but of ill health, in Malvern in 1294, and although his body was buried 'before the image of St Giles' in Little Malvern Priory, his heart returned home to Coberly to rest in the south wall of the chancel. This stone memorial records his heart burial, the only one in the Cotswolds. Directly behind this spot and on the outside of the church beside the path, lies his faithful horse Lombard, whom he dearly loved.

Giles' son, Thomas, followed in his father's footsteps, fighting in the battle of Crécy, and returning to rebuild this church before his own death in about 1350. He too lies here, in the south chapel. By his side is his wife Joan, who later married Sir William Whittington, and bore her famous son Richard, three times lord mayor of London. It is thought that Richard spent some of his childhood here in Coberly.

*OTHER PLACES
OF INTEREST*

*Elkstone Church to
the south (p. 43);
Crickley Hill
Country Park to the
west; Devil's
Chimney,
Leckhampton, to
the north.*

DAGLINGWORTH

A Medieval Dovecote

31

Location: 3 miles
north-west of
Cirencester off
A417 (the Ermine
Way)

MAP REFERENCE:
163: 996046

Hiding behind the trees in the private grounds of the one-time manor at Lower End is this fine circular medieval dovecote. Said to be the second oldest in the country, it was built by the Godstow nuns. It has nesting holes for 500 birds and it still has its revolving ladder, or potence, by which they may be reached. The medieval builder obviously gave more thought than was usual in the cote's building, for he added a string course to prevent rats climbing into the nesting boxes.

Daglingworth Church a short distance away contains some fine Saxon sculpture, including a small Crucifixion. This is unusual in that Christ is accompanied by two Roman soldiers, one holding a spear and the other the sponge of vinegar. Sometimes the church is locked.

OTHER PLACES
OF INTEREST

Sapperton to the
south-west (p. 90);
Cirencester to the
south-east (p. 24).

DEERHURST

A Saxon Priory Church

The priory church of St Mary was once part of a rich Benedictine monastery which owned 30,000 acres in Gloucestershire, mainly in the ancient kingdom of Hwicce. It is now the only surviving Anglo-Saxon monastic church in England. Over the years it has been added to and now has, astonishingly, seventeen doorways, many of different ages and at different levels. The church is plain and severe in spite of its gargoyles and memorials.

There is much to see, and an excellent guidebook points out items of interest, such as the unique tub-like carved Saxon font, and the holes high in the walls near the altar where ancient builders inserted their wooden scaffolding. It is recorded that the church was also the scene of a meeting between Canute and Edmund Ironside in 1016 when they discussed the treaty whereby Canute became King of England.

DEERHURST

Her Faithful Friend

The brass to Sir John and Lady Alice Cassey can be found at the east end of the north aisle in the priory church. Measuring 7 ft 5 in x 3 ft 1 in, it is by no means the only brass memorial in Gloucestershire, but it is unique and across the centuries dog-lovers must have warmed to Lady Alice. Since 1400 Alice has lain beside her husband, her hands folded in prayer, a small plaited cap, a 'fret . . . next to her hair', like Chaucer's lady in his 'Legend of a Good Woman'; but half-hidden at Alice's feet crouches her dog Terri. The dog, so carefully incised by the

craftsman, thought to be a greyhound and complete down to his collar of bells, must have been the lady's close and much-loved companion, for nowhere else can such a memorial be found. This is the earliest and now the only named dog to be so portrayed in the country – a brass at Ingham in Norfolk formerly commemorated another dog, Jakki.

DEERHURST

For My Brother Elfric

eerhurst is unique in having not only a Saxon minster, now a parish church, but also a Saxon chapel. The small chapel, down a path 200 yards away from St Mary's, was built by Odda, a kinsman of Edward the Confessor, in memory of his brother Elfric, and dedicated in 1056. The original stone is now in the Ashmolean Museum in Oxford, but a copy may be seen in the chapel, and beside it a verse written by the poet R.A. Hopwood (1868–1950), aptly entitled 'A Little Sanctuary'.

The Lombardic letters read:

Earl Odda had this royal hall built and dedicated in honour of the Holy Trinity for the good of the soul of his brother Elfric, which in this place quitted the body. Bishop Ealdrid dedicated it on 12 April, in the fourteenth year of the reign of Edward, King of the English.

Four months later, Odda himself died, and was buried near his brother at Pershore, now in Worcestershire.

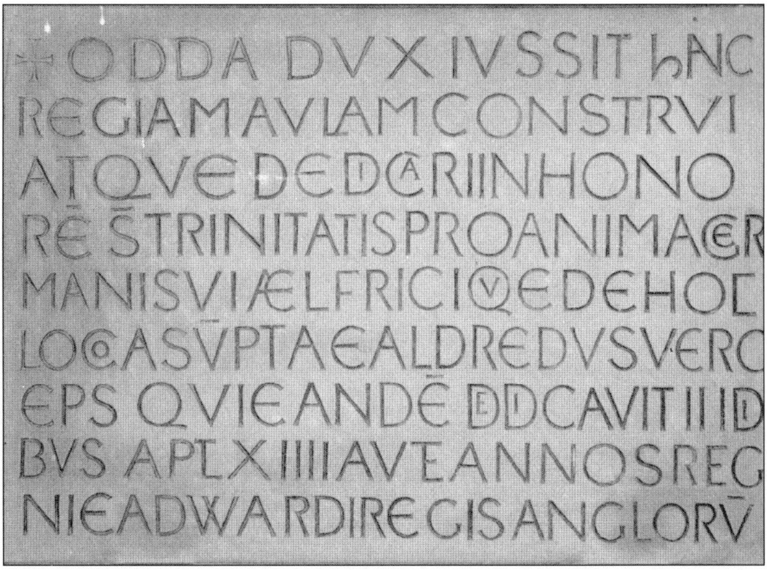

OTHER PLACES OF INTEREST

Tewkesbury to the north (p. 108); Ashleworth and Hartpury to the south-west (pp. 3, 61).

DIDMARTON

A Triple-decker Pulpit

Location: on the county border, 6 miles south-west of Tetbury on A433

MAP REFERENCE: 173: 822873

Few churches still boast of owning a triple-decker pulpit, but here at Didmarton one has been restored. In the medieval church of St Lawrence the pulpit, along with other eighteenth-century furnishings, show us what a country church was like in Georgian times. The parish clerk sat at the lower level leading the congregation in psalms and responses, while the minister conducted the service from the middle tier before ascending to stand beneath the sounding-board for the sermon. Situated as he would be here in the nave and facing the north transept, the minister was ideally placed to view all his congregation in their narrow box pews, as he exhorted them to better ways. On a sunny day, he must have been outlined in light like a messiah, for the pulpit is linked to large windows on either side by a framing arch. In the 1870s the Victorians chose to build another church, St Michael's, to the north, with the result that now St Lawrence's is little used and generally kept locked.

DIDMARTON

Hat Pegs for Giants?

It is rather difficult to photograph this double row of hat pegs in the old church of St Lawrence because, as is suggested by the illustration, they are so far above the floor. They form neat rows at eaves level at the west end of the nave. The explanation is disappointingly obvious. No giants here, after all, but a congregation which sat in a gallery, added, it is thought, in the eighteenth century. The 'non-giants' were probably musicians who accompanied the service, or others who, like those in a similar gallery in the north transept, could not afford to rent the box pews below.

On the outside of the south wall can be seen where a door once led to stairs reaching the gallery and these now redundant hat pegs.

OTHER PLACES OF INTEREST

Tetbury (p. 105), and Westonbirt Arboretum to the north-east.

DOVER'S HILL

The Cotswold Olimpicks

Location: *1 mile
north-west of
Chipping Campden*

MAP REFERENCE:
151: 137398

From Dover's Hill, owned since 1928 by the National Trust, one has breathtaking views stretching from the Malverns to the Vale of Evesham, Worcestershire and Warwickshire. For most of the year only walkers share the hill with grazing sheep, birds and the moles tunnelling beneath it, but every summer the area rings to the sound of the 'Cotswold Olimpicks', a meeting which began three centuries ago.

The games, first held in 1612, were the idea of Robert Dover (1582–1652), a lawyer who had come from Norfolk. He opened his 'Olimpicks' in great style. Decked out in fine clothes and astride a white horse, he fired a cannon from a mock castle specially erected each year. Various rustic sports began, as this sketched copy of the sixteenth-century woodcut shows: horse racing, coursing, jumping, throwing the sledgehammer, fencing, wrestling, pitching the bar and even shin kicking. The fun was enjoyed by all, is mentioned by Shakespeare and continued until 1852 when the event's popularity led to great crowds and unruly behaviour. A hundred years later the 'Olimpicks' were revived and are now an annual event each June.

OTHER PLACES
OF INTEREST

*Kiftsgate Stone
(overleaf).*

DOVER'S HILL

An Original 'Moot' Point

*Location: ½ mile
south of Dover's
Hill car park beside
the road to
Willersley*
MAP REFERENCE:
151: 142390

South of Dover's Hill stands the Kiftsgate Stone. For centuries Dover's Hill was the traditional site for the meetings of the Court of the Hundred of Kiftsgate. Deriving from the Old English 'gemot', a meeting, this was the 'moot' point – the meeting place for all to gather to hear important news and to discuss events. It is remembered by the Kiftsgate Stone, thought to be pre-Saxon, the hole in it perfectly round and possibly the place where Saxon chiefs rested their swords while counselling their serfs or collecting dues. In a later century, the proclamation of George III was made here. Now the stone, just inside a private wood on the right beside the road to Willersley, is yet another silent reminder of the history which is all round us if we know where to look for it.

*OTHER PLACES
OF INTEREST*

*Chipping Campden
to the east (p. 20);
Dover's Hill
(previous page).*

DUMBLETON

A Primitive Green Man

Location: south of
A435 Evesham to
Cheltenham road, at
the northern edge of
the county
MAP REFERENCE:
150: 018358

This strange little figure has looked upon everyone entering St Peter's Church for hundreds of years. Set on the tympanum, he is a primitive green man, a common Romanesque motif, but one in exceptional condition, and one of the surviving features, along with the nave and the chancel, of the original Norman church. He has surveyed many alterations to the building through the centuries, ranging from the addition of the thirteenth-century tower, the six bells in 1729 and the south porch in 1905.

Inside St Peter's, the earliest memorial is to Elizabeth I's courtier, Sir Charles Percy, who rode hotfoot in 1603 to James I in Edinburgh with news of the queen's death. As lord of the manor of Dumbleton, he kneels, a somewhat chunky figure, resplendent beside his wife Dorothy and their baby Anne. He died in 1628 and at Dorothy's later death, the manor passed to Sir Richard and Lady Susannah Cocks. Their memorial, recording their family history in detail, graces the wall opposite Sir Charles.

OTHER PLACES
OF INTEREST

Hailes Abbey and
Stanway to the
south-east (pp. 60,
96); Winchcombe to
the south (p. 113);
Broadway Country
Park to the east.

DYMOCK

Where Daffodils Run 'in Golden Tides'

Dymock, in the centre of Gloucestershire's 'Daffodil Crescent', a village whose name has been spelt a dozen different ways, proudly displays evidence of 2,000 years of its history inside St Mary's Church behind Wintour's Green. It also records with pride the work of the Dymock poets. Between 1911 and 1914 Lascelles Abercrombie, John Drinkwater, Rupert Brooke, W.W. Gibson, Edward Thomas and Robert Frost

lived in this area, extolling its beauty; these were friends who shared a love of verse and the spoken word. War came, and the group broke up, carrying their poetry away with them, but there can be no doubt that this little village had influenced their work.

(The 'Daffodil Crescent' runs from Bromsberrow to Flaxley, through Dymock, and just above Newent and Huntley, forming a curve through the north and west of the area.)

DYMOCK

The Old Cottage

Here we see just a small part of Dymock's past, an almost perfect example of a cruck cottage dwelling. Noted as a building of special architectural interest, it is one of very few left in England, although in the fifteenth century when this was a common method of building, it was an everyday sight. Now probably over 500 years old, and altered in the late nineteenth and early twentieth centuries, it is well maintained and, of course, as a private residence, a cottage to be admired as we pass through Dymock. The house stands opposite the village school which was established by Ann Cam in 1825, but that's another story.

DYMOCK

The Dymock Curse

Spells and charms were once very much part of life, and here we have proof that they existed in Gloucestershire. This unique example, reproduced here by courtesy of the Gloucester Folk Museum, is a curse which was called down on Sarah Ellis during the second half of the seventeenth century. It is scratched on thin lead just over 3 in square, and is thought to have been based on an occult

book translated into English in 1651. The symbols below Sarah's name, written backwards, probably represent spirits of the Moon, and the names those of Demons. After the number 369, it reads:

> Hasmodat, Acteus, Magalesius, Ormenus, Lieus, Nicon, Mimon, Zeper,
> Make this person to Banish away from this place and Countery Amen.
> To my desier Amen

It was found lying hidden under the sill inside a tiny cupboard beside a chimney in Wilton Place in Dymock, during renovations in 1892. No-one knows who Sarah Ellis was, although local legend speaks of a girl at that time who committed suicide and was buried at a crossroads with a stake in her heart. Indeed, 2½ miles from Wilton Place, on the parish boundary, there is said to be a place called Ellis Cross.

OTHER PLACES OF INTEREST

Newent and Three Choirs Vineyard to the south (pp. 71, 73).

ELKSTONE

A Priest's Dovecote

Location: 1 mile
east of A417, 6
miles south of
Cheltenham
MAP REFERENCE:
163: 968123

Behind this narrow doorway, near the pulpit in St John's Church, lies a flight of twenty-eight tiny circular stone steps which lead up into a columbarium or dovecote above the chancel. This feature is rare and the cote, although small by some standards, holds more than forty nest-holes.

The church, at 900 ft the highest in the Cotswolds, dates from about 1160. Its Norman work is much valued, especially the lovely double chancel arch with zigzag carving. Here the boss features an unusual belt and buckle in its design, thought to have been added to give a feeling of security to those standing beneath its heavy stonework.

Elkstone was mentioned in the Domesday Book and derives from 'the stone of Ealac', referring to a Saxon stone or stone building. It is thought that a small stone set against the wall of the vestry could possibly be the stone which gave this village its name.

*OTHER PLACES
OF INTEREST*

*Syde to the south-
west (p. 103).*

EPNEY

Location: 8 miles
south of Gloucester
off A38, down a
narrow road, over
Parkend Bridge and
just beyond the new
flood barriers on the
Severn

MAP REFERENCE:
162: 111765

A Surfeit of . . . Eels

This unassuming and mundane-looking façade conceals something very interesting which happens every spring. Between March and May huge tanks are filled with tiny elvers waiting to complete their long journey which ends in their restocking fish farms throughout the country. Spawned nearly three years earlier, the size of a matchstick and transparent, these tiny creatures travel with the Gulf Stream from their spawning grounds in the Caribbean, only to land in the nets of local fishermen who supply the fishery here. Fishing is carried out at night. Nets 3 ft long and 18 in deep are pegged down about 3 ft below the surface of the water when the tide is ebbing, and lanterns behind them attract the

elvers. The catches vary, but in a good year between two and three tons of elvers may pass through the depot. Although there are two others elsewhere, this fishery is the oldest elver-collecting centre in the country. Confiscated from the Germans during the Second World War, the ministry offered it, in 1947, to Mr George Clarke, who worked in eels in Billingsgate Fish Market. Still a family business, the fishery takes its name from the village of Saul ¼ mile away.

OTHER PLACES
OF INTEREST

Slimbridge to the
south; Stroud to the
south-east.

FAIRFORD

Come, See My Scriptures in Glass

*Location: 8 miles
east of Cirencester
in the south-east
corner of the
Cotswolds*

MAP REFERENCE:
163: 152012

S ince about 1490 this strange little figure has been looking over his shoulder, as he clambers up on to the string course of the parapet of St Mary's Church at Fairford. This jester is one of the many reliefs, carvings and grotesques which decorate the external walls of this handsome wool church. It was built in the late 1400s by wealthy wool merchant John Tame, a fervent supporter and friend of the Tudor kings. It is thought that Henry VII may have been the donor of the unique windows which make Fairford church famous. They make up the only complete medieval set to have survived in the British Isles, and covering an area of more than 2,000 sq ft. They are known as 'the poor man's Bible', portraying as they do the story of the Christian faith. Henry VIII is said to have admired them when he stayed with the Tame family in 1520, and with the help of an excellent leaflet in the church, the modern visitor may also try to interpret their glowing biblical scenes and their hidden royal portraits.

FAIRFORD

Pictures of the Past and a Treacle Bible

The misericord showing a woman attacking the dog who steals from a pot as she spins is yet another example of medieval art, art which here in Fairford shows a distinct sense of humour. The fourteen misericords in the chancel pre-date the church itself, and are thought to have been carved for Cirencester Abbey, dissolved in 1539. They depict various everyday scenes and creatures from the Old Testament. Whatever

their story, the seats would have been much welcomed by the monks who could lean against them as they sang their daily offices. The word 'misericord' derives from the Latin *misere* or mercy.

Fairford Church also owns a rare bible dated 1551, known as the 'treacle' bible. Its translator, one Thomas Mathew, when working on chapter eight of Jeremiah, referred not to 'balm' in Gilead, as did the later Authorised Version, but wrote '. . . for there is no more tryacle at Gilead'. The bible is now in safe keeping elsewhere.

OTHER PLACES OF INTEREST

Cotswold Water Park to the south-west; Lechlade to the east (p. 63); Bibury to the north-west (p. 10).

FARMINGTON

A Horse-lover's Gate

*Location: 1¼ miles
north-east of
Northleach, on a
minor road off
A429 (Fosse Way)*

MAP REFERENCE:
163: 136153

Whoever was responsible for this gate at St Peter's Church showed great originality in its design. It consists of ninety horseshoes welded together. The church, basically Norman, is set deep in the countryside, and in nearby fields horses graze – perhaps horses from whose family these horseshoes originally came!

St Peter's also has an older, unusual and sometimes missed feature in its late Perpendicular tower. Each clock face has only one long metal finger and the dials are of stone with the now fading numerals painted on.

The attractive village green has an octagonal shelter dedicated to one Edward Waller in 1822, and a circular stone dovecote rounds off the charming features to be found here.

*OTHER PLACES
OF INTEREST*

*Bourton-on-the-
Water to the north
(p. 13); Great
Barrington to the
east (p. 57).*

FLAXLEY

Location: west of
A48, 1½ miles
north-east of
Littledean, near
Flaxley Abbey
MAP REFERENCE:
162: 674163

St Anthony's Well

S ome distance from Flaxley Abbey, among woods now owned by the Forestry Commission, and overhung by beeches, one finds the secluded well of St Anthony. In common with other wells of its type, its pure spring water was said to have healing properties, and it does contain iron and lime from the strata through which it rises. The monks of the nearby abbey were among the first to use it. On their advice, those suffering from skin diseases bathed in the well water (average temperature 50°C) on each of the first nine mornings in May. Their success rate is not recorded, but legend has it that the waters were used in the eighteenth century, too, by pet owners who believed its properties would cure their dogs of mange or distemper. Evidently it was not only pet owners who continued to visit the well, for at the beginning of the nineteenth century the worn stone which now surrounds it was placed there 'for the convenience of bathers'.

Paul Felix

OTHER PLACES
OF INTEREST

Cinderford and
Littledean (p. 64) to
the south;
Westbury-on-Severn
to the south-east (p.
112); Mitcheldean
to the north.

Forest of Dean

The Speech House

Location: 3½ miles
south-west of
Cinderford on
B4226

MAP REFERENCE:
162: 620120

Within this building, now an hotel, are maintained traditions stretching back 900 years into Gloucestershire's past. When the house was built during the reign of Charles II in 1676, it was known as King's Lodge. It is set in the centre of the beautiful Forest of Dean, a royal hunting forest from the time of Canute in 1016, and created England's first forest park in 1938. The Speech House, extended over the years, is so called because since the seventeenth century it has been the building where the courts are held by the Verderers of Dean – the place where Speech Courts are held. The office of verderer, said to have been instituted by Canute, is an elected one and held for life. Their duties have always been to guard the 'vert and venison' for the king and to oversee all business within the forest. The court still meets four times a year in the court room, now a dining room, and although they no longer exercise their still legal powers against offenders, the verderers continue to fulfil an administrative role, and in so doing, continue a unique and ancient tradition, matched only, perhaps, by the Freeminers of Dean who also meet here occasionally.

OTHER PLACES
OF INTEREST
Coleford and
Newland (p. 74) to
the south-west;
Newnham on
Severn to the east
(p. 76).

FORTHAMPTON

*Location: 2 miles
west of Tewkesbury
and south of A438
to Ledbury*
MAP REFERENCE:
150: 859325

Unnecessary Stocks?

A set of stocks for three and a whipping post at the foot of the path rising to the church of St Mary the Virgin, are found in a little village where, it would appear, good behaviour was the norm. There is only one written record of their being used, and that in the year 1788 when they were probably about a year old. One Mr Newman was paid 7/6d for whiping (sic) Katherine Attwood. She was a problem in the community it would seem, for it is also recorded that the village had to care for her two illegitimate children. Perhaps she was ducked in Pound Pond nearby as well.

The church pre-dates the stocks by more than five centuries. A devil's-face keystone, probably Saxon, leers down at visitors from above the door and inside, a thirteenth-century stone altar still stands secure on its stone legs – a rare feature, since most of these were removed at the Reformation.

*OTHER PLACES
OF INTEREST*

*Deerhurst to the
south-east (p. 32);
Tewkesbury to the
east (p. 108).*

GLOUCESTER

The First War Memorial

The Great East Window in Gloucester Cathedral could be said to be the country's first and perhaps finest war memorial. It is the largest stained glass window in England and still contains its original glass. Standing 72 ft high and 38 ft wide, it was erected in about 1350 by Lord Bradeston, Governor of Gloucester Castle, as a memorial to his friend Sir Maurice Berkeley who was killed, along with other shire knights, during the French campaign of 1346–7, a campaign which included the battle of Crécy and the siege of Calais. It depicts full-length figures with their emblems and the Christ in Majesty surrounded by angels.

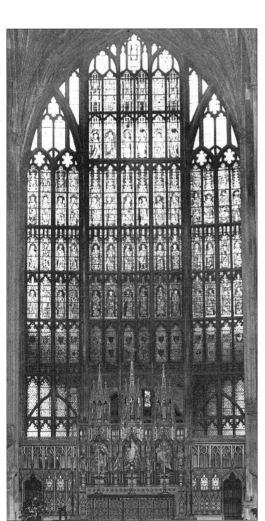

Jack Farley

GLOUCESTER

The Monks at Play

Beneath the window, and under seats in the choir hide fourteenth-century monastic misericords, fifty-eight in all, showing life centuries ago and here depicting two boys playing ball. But look further and evidence may be found of other, less energetic pastimes.

In the north side of the cloisters, that lovely stonework said to be a fine example of 'the earliest fan vaulting in the country', we can just see, scratched on the stone benches which acted as seats, two sets of lines. These lines form the squares and patterns needed to play games like Nine Men's Morris and Fox and Geese. They are, as the photograph below shows, now almost too faint to record. It is generally thought that they were scratched there centuries ago by young monks, whiling away their time in some of their few idle moments, but they add a human touch to the recording of Gloucester's past history.

GLOUCESTER

Bishop Hooper's House

This impressive late fifteenth-century merchant's house on the far left is thought to have once been home to Bishop Hooper, one of the first Protestant martyrs to die for his faith during the bloody five-year reign of Queen Mary. John Hooper, born in Somerset in 1495, the son of a country gentleman, was an Oxford graduate who became a Cistercian monk before accepting the post of bishop for the new joint Diocese of Worcester and Gloucester in 1552. The following year he was arrested as a heretic by Catholic Mary, and after a long imprisonment, was burned alive near the church of St Mary de Lode not far from his home.

Today the house, along with its neighbours, forms the fascinating Folk Museum. Within this lovely Tudor building, with its startlingly uneven floors, one finds a sixteenth-century wall painting, a seventeenth-century wooden water main and a Victorian schoolroom among many other excellent exhibits. Anyone wishing to savour something of Gloucestershire's past could do no better than begin here.

GLOUCESTER

Centuries of Welcome

Here is another of Gloucester's interesting buildings. The New Inn is tucked away, but leave the busy modern street and step into its courtyard, and one literally steps back into history. Beautifully maintained, and now owned by Berni Inns, this medieval inn has been in constant use since about 1350, when pilgrims stayed here while visiting the shrine of Edward II (murdered in 1357 at Berkeley Castle), in St Peter's Abbey, now Gloucester Cathedral. Extended by John Twining, a monk,

who named it the New Inn, the yard and galleries were later probably used by strolling players for their performances in Tudor times. It was further extended when it became an important coaching inn in the eighteenth century. Here in the courtyard, its history breathes all around you, and you would not be at all surprised to see an Elizabethan walk along the gallery before disappearing into one of the bedrooms above.

GLOUCESTER

Where Once Were Bells

Anyone using the post office, built in 1927, may not realize that it replaces a business which was very important in Gloucestershire's past. This was the site of a bell foundry, owned by Abraham Rudhall, the most famous maker of church bells in England. Founded in 1684, the family business cast more than 4,000 bells over the next century and a half, and many of them still ring out across the shires. One of the oldest is at Oddington, near Stow. It is estimated that one out of every three bells in Gloucestershire was made here, as well as some of those in Westminster Abbey and in various cathedrals. The foundry closed down in 1848.

GLOUCESTER

Location: at the junction of Northgate, Southgate, Eastgate and Westgate streets

British (Isles) Time

This clock, unlike much of Gloucester, has yet to reach its first century, but it is included because it is unusual and because it represents the local craftsmanship which was once part of ship-building. The figures were the work of craftsmen from a local firm which carved figureheads for sailing ships. The clock was made in 1904 and shows Father Time, complete with scythe, poised to strike the great bell. He is flanked by a rather complacent-looking John Bull, Miss Ireland with her harp, a Scottish piper and Miss Wales.

OTHER PLACES OF INTEREST

The many museums in the dock area; Great Witcombe Roman villa to the south-east; Ashleworth, Hartpury, Maisemore (pp. 3, 61, 69) to the north.

GREAT BARRINGTON

Never to Draw Sword Again

Location: 6 miles
south-east of
Bourton-on-the-
Water along minor
road off A424

MAP REFERENCE:
163: 206135

At first glance there may seem little unusual in this effigy to a late Tudor knight in the old church of St Mary the Virgin at Great Barrington. Tucked away in the north aisle beside the organ, his stone beginning to crumble with time, Captain Edmond Bray has lain since 1620, with his sword on his right side. He was not left handed. He is believed to have been present at the camp at Tilbury before the Armada in 1588, where anticipation of battle and excitement made passions run high. Here, it is said, in the heat of the moment he drew his sword and killed a man. Queen Elizabeth, who visited the camp to give her stirring 'I know I have the body of a weak and feeble woman' speech, heard of the incident, but pardoned Bray. So grateful was he for her lenience that he vowed never again to act impetuously or to draw sword again with his right hand. History does not record whether he kept his word, but his effigy suggests that he did.

GREAT BARRINGTON

For a Fisherman

Across the nave from Captain Bray in the church of St Mary the Virgin, and inside the chancel arch, another more modern tablet records a man who is remembered, not for the legend of an accident but for what must have been his love of a more peaceful pursuit. The words speak for themselves and are an original, yet still loving, way of remembering someone. However, although Charles Wingfield's life is recorded through his fishing, he belonged to a family who certainly played their part in war. A marble tablet at the rear of the church records the death

GOD GRANT THAT I MAY FISH
UNTIL MY DYING DAY
AND WHEN IT COMES TO MY LAST CAST,
I HUMBLY PRAY
WHEN IN THE LORD'S SAFE LANDING NET
I'M PEACEFULLY ASLEEP,
THAT IN HIS MERCY
I BE JUDGED AS GOOD ENOUGH TO KEEP.

CHARLES JOHN FITZROY RHYS WINGFIELD

of another member of the family who died at Ypres in 1915, and the name appears again four times in a Roll of Honour. The Wingfield home is Barrington Park; the buildings are next to the church and were built in the mid-1730s for Earl Talbot. They replace the manor house which was burnt down at that time, and which had once been the home of Sir Edmond Bray and his family. Barrington Park is a private residence and neither it nor the grounds is open to the public.

OTHER PLACES OF INTEREST

Little Barrington to the south; Farmington (p. 47) and Northleach (p. 80) to the west.

GUITING POWER

Maintaining the Breeds

Location: 5 miles west of Stow-on-the-Wold on B4077

MAP REFERENCE:
163: 111268

Here is a pig, a Gloucester Old Spot, which very much prefers a natural lifestyle. The breed is now very rare (less than 170 females are left), because it is not suited to modern intensive farming methods, preferring to live out of doors and create its own nest. This minority breed, with its lop ears and once known as the Orchard Pig, evolved in Berkeley Vale and was used for both pork and bacon. Legend said that the spots were bruises from fallen apples and that the pork would

taste of cider. But here at Cotswold Farm Park, in its twenty-fifth season and devoted to the preservation of old breeds, the Gloucester Old Spot rootles happily beside many other unique and historic animals including Cotswold sheep, Gloucester cattle and Shire horses. Their survival is due partly to the excellent work begun here by Joe Henson, founder chairman of the Rare Breeds Survival Trust, who had the foresight to create this living heritage on Bemborough Farm.

The farm is open daily from 1 April to 1 October, and includes a pets' corner and a farm nature trail.

OTHER PLACES OF INTEREST

Bourton (p. 13), the Slaughters (p. 66) and Stow-on-the-Wold (p. 99) to the east; Sudeley (p. 101) and Winchcombe (p. 113) to the west.

HAILES ABBEY

'The blood of Crist that is in Hales'

Chaucer, *Pardoner's Tale*, l. 652

Location: 2 miles north-east of Winchcombe

MAP REFERENCE:
150: 150300

In the thirteenth-century Hailes Abbey, as well as being home and place of worship to the abbot, monks and lay brothers, was also an important place of pilgrimage, for it housed a shrine said to contain a phial of the holy blood of Christ. Among the last of the Cistercian abbeys, it was founded in 1246, consecrated five years later, and built with money given

by Henry III's brother Richard, Earl of Cornwall, as thanksgiving for having survived a shipwreck. It became the twelfth richest Cistercian abbey in England until, in 1539, it fell victim to Henry VIII's edicts and was dissolved. Even though only the shell remains today, it is easy to see that Hailes must always have been an impressive building. Now a ruin encircled by great chestnut trees, it still breathes an air of majesty and peace to be enjoyed by the thousands of visitors who make a modern pilgrimage just to see it.

The abbey is cared for by English Heritage and the National Trust and is open all year round apart from Mondays in winter. A museum beside it gives its full history.

*OTHER PLACES
OF INTEREST*

Hailes Church across the road from the abbey; Stanway House to the north (p. 96); Winchcombe to the south (p. 113).

HARTPURY

An Ancient Home for Bees

61

*Location: 1½ miles
south of Hartpury
village off A417*

MAP REFERENCE:
162: 790228

Here, now, in the private grounds of Hartpury College at Murrell's End near Gloucester, sits the oldest beehouse in England. Built before 1500, it is a handsome edifice of carved stone, 30 ft long and 8 ft high and providing niches for twenty-eight hives, and it is a reminder of the importance of honey as a food and sweetener in the days before sugar was easily obtainable. It originally stood at Nailsworth, the property, it is thought, of the Abbaye aux Dames which had received the Manor of Minchinhampton from William the Conqueror. By 1968 the land on which the beehouse stood had become part of a police station, and so it was carefully dismantled by the Stroud branch of the Gloucester Beekeepers' Association and reassembled here. The Hartpury College of Agriculture, Horticulture and other land-based industries is a fitting place for such a unique feature, and one hopes the beehouse will remain safe and protected for many centuries to come.

*OTHER PLACES
OF INTEREST*

*Gloucester and
Maisemore to the
south (pp. 51, 69);
Ashleworth to the
north (p. 3).*

KEMPLEY

Location: 5 miles
north-west of
Newent and 1 mile
north of Kempley
itself
MAP REFERENCE:
149: 671296

Frescoes for a Father

Just north of Kempley and surrounded by rich meadows lies the eleventh-century church of St Mary. It is home to a set of medieval wall paintings said to be the finest in Britain.

The church was built by Hugh de Lacy on the site of a Saxon church in memory of his father Walter who died in May 1085, and who is actually buried in Gloucester Cathedral. It is thought that the cortège rested here in the old Saxon church on its journey to Gloucester from Hereford, where Walter had fallen to his death from the battlements of St Peter's Church which he had just built. Having rebuilt St Mary's here, Hugh commissioned some frescoes, the best of which still glow a brick red in the gloom of the chancel 900 years later. True frescoes, the colour having been applied to wet plaster so that it was absorbed to become permanent, the paintings show the Apostles, Christ in Majesty, the Virgin, saints and cherubim, and two figures thought to be Hugh and his father.

The now redundant St Mary's, which is in the care of English Heritage, also boasts the earliest surviving parish church roof in the country.

OTHER PLACES OF INTEREST

Dymock to the north-east (p. 40); Much Marcle (Hereford and Worcester) to the north-west.

LECHLADE

Old Father Thames

Location: in the
south-east corner of
the county, at the
crossing of A361
and A417

MAP REFERENCE:
163: 223990

Old Father Thames now reclines at St John's Lock, below St John's Bridge on the A417, in the south-west corner of the county. He rests in a suitably historic place, for this lock is the first and the highest of the navigable locks on the Thames. Looking very like Neptune, and sculpted by Rafaelle Monti, he was originally commissioned by the Merchants of London for the Crystal Palace Exhibition of 1851. From 1958 to 1974 he marked the head of the Thames in a field near Cirencester and then, for safety, he was moved here, presented by Mr H. Scott Freeman, a conservator of the Thames.

St John's Bridge, although turnpiked in the eighteenth century, should not be confused with Halfpenny Bridge to the west. There, too, tolls were collected at its little square tollhouse until the late 1880s.

The sculpture may be reached by water or road, or via a walk across fields and a causeway from Shelley's Walk at the back of St Lawrence's Church.

*OTHER PLACES
OF INTEREST*

*Buscot House
(National Trust), to
the south-east;
Fairford (p. 45) to
the west ; Bibury
(p. 10) to the north-
west.*

Location: 1½ miles
east of Cinderford
on A48
MAP REFERENCE:
162: 672136

LITTLEDEAN

A Deliberate Mistake?

Many check the time by Littledean's church clock without noticing the mistake in its figures; but it would seem that the error is now viewed with pride by the villagers, for it has never been corrected. Indeed, the figures were recently regilded, still incorrect. The clock sits in the old tower of the church of St Ethelbert, a small, mainly thirteenth-century building sheltering behind its wall beside the busy main road. An old iron footscraper stands beside the door and inside Norman pillars bear some interesting shamrock carvings. Nowadays, however, the church is often kept locked.

LITTLEDEAN

House With a Past

S ituated just outside Littledean on the Newnham Road, Littledean Hall, set in 50 acres of park and gardens, broods on its past. Once the manor of the lords of Dene, and known to have been lived in continuously from before the Norman Conquest, this great house, added to and altered over the years, is said to be one of England's oldest houses. No-one is surprised to learn that it is reputed to be haunted. The dining room was the scene of murder and intrigue in the Civil War, and there are other ghostly tales a-plenty too.

The present hall stands on Roman foundations, and recent excavations have revealed a Roman temple in the gardens. Nearby, in spring, primroses bloom in the foundations of a medieval ironworks, the earliest so far excavated in the Forest of Dean, probably dating back to the Saxons and also yielding examples of twelfth- and fifteenth-century artefacts. Apart from the history surrounding this great house, there are pleasant walks and panoramic views to enjoy. A private residence, the hall is open to the public daily from April to October. Check a tourist centre for details.

*OTHER PLACES
OF INTEREST*

*Cinderford and the
Forest of Dean
(p. 49) to the north;
Newnham on
Severn (p. 76) to the
south; Blaize Bailey
picnic site to the
south.*

Location: 1 mile
north of Bourton-
on-the-Water
MAP REFERENCE:
163: 168226

LOWER SLAUGHTER

The Village Mill

At the top of the village of Lower Slaughter stands this now disused mill, its red brick chimney a striking contrast to the neat row of low Cotswold stone cottages beside it. Waters tumble through the mill race, but the iron wheel is still. There had probably been a mill on this site for centuries – Slaughter Mill is referred to in documents of 1502. By 1735 it was separated from the manorial estate, and this building was erected in the nineteenth century. By 1879 it was run by the Wilkins family, under whose name it still traded in 1961. About this time it became a bakery, but this too has now gone. The tall chimney suggests that steam as well as water power was used here.

Lower Slaughter, with its neighbouring Upper village, is pretty and much more attractive than its name would suggest; but 'Slaughter' derives from 'slohtre' meaning 'marshy place' and evidence of this is more obvious in the Upper area.

LOWER SLAUGHTER

Cotswold Home for One Thousand

Looking at this pretty Cotswold stone house, one might wonder at its tiny door and lack of lower windows. Perfect in every other respect, externally at least, it was built in the fifteenth century and is set at the edge of the grounds of the manor house, itself built in 1658 for the High Sheriff of Gloucestershire, and now a Grade Two listed building and an exclusive hotel and restaurant. The house is not an annexe to the main

building. It is, and always has been, a dovecote, and it stands here as it has for centuries, unaltered but well maintained, and with nesting boxes for more than one thousand birds. It is one of the largest and most important of its time and, in its unusual design, certainly unique. It is the oldest part of the buildings in these grounds, for the stable block to the east was built in about 1770.

OTHER PLACES OF INTEREST

Bourton-on-the-Water (p. 13) to the south; Stow-on-the-Wold (p. 99) to the north; Wyck Rissington (p. 118) to the east.

*Location: 1 mile
west of Stow down
a lane off the B4068*
MAP REFERENCE:
163: 174258

LOWER SWELL

A Striking Bell Turret

T he unusual arrangement of flywheels standing high above St Mary's
Church is what may first attract the attention of the visitor driving
along the peaceful country lanes of Lower Swell. This bell turret
was built as recently as 1901, when the old bell was rehung with two new
ones to celebrate the 51-year ministry of the Revd David Royce, who had
initiated the church's enlargement after his arrival as vicar there in 1850.
Inside the church, however, the visitor will be rewarded by seeing a fine
Norman chancel arch consisting of twenty-six sculpted stones which show
some of the finest Norman carving in the county. The original Norman
building here was first called a chapel, and its earliest recorded minister
was appointed in 1282.

*OTHER PLACES
OF INTEREST*

*The Slaughters to
the south (p. 66);
Cotswold Farm
Park to the west.*

MAISEMORE

Bridge With a History

This wide, sweeping, busy bridge, leading from Gloucester and into the Leadon Vale, is the modern version of an historic crossing point over the Severn. Completed in June 1956, it replaces at least six others which have stood here. The first recorded bridge was built in about the year 1200 by William Fitz Anketil, and during the following centuries one subsequent bridge was 'cut down by Royalist besiegers' (1643), and another neglected by parishioners who were fined £200 in 1709 for not repairing it. William is remembered on a large stone cross, which originally stood at St Mary's Church in Gloucester, a cross he himself made 'in honour of Our Lord Jesus Christ Who was crucified for us'. The cross also tells us that 'the same William Fitz Anketil began this bridge of Maisemore'.

*OTHER PLACES
OF INTEREST*

*Ashleworth (p. 3),
Gloucester
(pp. 51–6) and
Hartpury (p. 61) to
the north; Rudford
(p. 87) to the west.*

MORETON IN MARSH

A Toll Board

Location: 3 miles
north of Stow at the
meeting of the A44
and the A429
MAP REFERENCE:
151: 205325

At one time traders were left in no doubt about how much it would cost them to spend a day in Moreton. Such charges were probably worth paying, for this still busy market town on the Fosse Way was once a meeting point for four counties, as marked by the Four Shires Stone two miles away to the east on the A44. 'Marsh' is a corruption of 'march', meaning boundary. The board is placed on the High Street wall of the Curfew Tower. This building was erected in the sixteenth century at the junction with what is now Oxford Street, and is probably Moreton's oldest building. The curfew bell, dated 1633, was rung morning and evening until 1860, having been endowed by one Sir Robert Fry who had found its ringing had helped to guide him home in the fog. The origin of a curfew dates back to Norman times when a bell was rung to warn people to 'cover fire' for the night.

THE UNDERMENTIONED TOLLS.

Will be charged in the Market Town of Moreton in Marsh on all market, fair and other days on and after this date.

Roundabouts driven by steam prohibited.

For every	Roundabout driven by pony	5's.to 6's.per day
	Shooting Gallery.	5's.to 7's.6d.
	Cocoanut Shoot..	2's.6d.
	Cheap John Cart.	2's.6d.
	Swing.	2s.6d. to 5s.0d.
	Waggon.	1's.0d.
	Cart.	6d.
	Hand Cart.	3d.
	Stall of whatever length.	
	1d. per foot minimum.	6d.

For Earthenware Dealers 1s.for the use of 12 sqr. yards or less and for every additional yard 1d.

For every Show, Menagerie, Bazzar, &c. not hereinbefore mentioned 1d. per square yard.

For every Caravan accompanying any of the Shows, Stalls, &c. and standing in the street 1's. per day, nothing to be allowed to stand within 18 feet of the Brick Pavement.

Residents having a stall in front of their Houses 5's. per year.   BY ORDER.

JOHN KENNEDY. Agent for,

THE RIGHT HON. LORD REDESDALE. K.C.V.O., C.B.
Lord of the Manor.

F.PAGE
Collector.

August 5th 1905.

OTHER PLACES
OF INTEREST

On the Broadway
Road, Wellington
Aviation Museum;
Batsford Arboretum
to the north-west;
Sezincote House
and gardens to the
west.

NEWENT

Victorian Newent

*Location: 9 miles
north-west of
Gloucester*

MAP REFERENCE:
162: 722269

A s well as admiring a striking seventeenth-century half-timbered Market House and old inns, the visitor to Newent may literally wander round Victorian shops and a network of cobbled streets. The Shambles Museum is a fascinating reconstruction of part of a Victorian town. It includes a pawn-shop, a variety of shops and workshops, a fully furnished four-storey house and a little tearoom where, if you were still paying turn of the century prices, you could enjoy a cup of coffee for ½*d* and plum cake for 1*d* – or bring your own jug and purchase the beverages for 1½*d* a pint!

The Chapmans, who describe themselves as 'natural collectors', began their museum eight years ago. It grew out of interest shown at various exhibitions they staged and gradually, as buildings round the main house became available, they have extended. Future plans include both an old-fashioned cottage garden and a Victorian vegetable garden beyond the existing streets.

NEWENT

A Tomb With a Mystery

ccording to the inscription on this impressive tomb in Newent churchyard, it is the last resting-place of Anna Edmonds who died, aged fifty-one, in 1867, her three small daughters who predeceased her and her husband Edmond. Anna died after falling downstairs, but some years later, rumours led to the circumstances of her death being reviewed, and suspicion fell on her husband. Her exhumation and subsequent post mortem – and exhumation so long after burial was extremely rare at that time – eventually led to Edmond's trial at the Old Bailey. He was finally acquitted, but the mystery does not end there. In spite of his name being on the tomb, his body, it is whispered by those who know, does not lie with his family. No-one knows how or where Edmond met his end, though it has been suggested that he died in poverty in London, having choked while in a rage. Anna and Edmond have taken the truth to the grave with them and the mysteries remain.

NEWENT

'Wine that Maketh Glad the Heart'

73

*Location: 1½ miles
north of Newent on
B4215*

MAP REFERENCE:
162: 778280

In the twelfth century William of Malmesbury wrote of Gloucestershire: 'No county in England has so many, or so good Vineyards', and happily the Three Choirs Vineyard near Newent has brought the past into the present by reviving this celebrated and ancient tradition. Started in 1973 with an experimental ½ acre, the business has rapidly expanded, so that now a wide variety of grapes is grown on the 'double curtain' trellis system over an area of more than 65 acres. This is now one of the six largest vineyards in Britain, a winner of many awards, and capable of producing over 250,000 bottles of pure and highly respected wines from grapes grown only in England. The red sandstone soil is particularly suited to vines, which are planted on well-drained south-facing slopes here in an area practically mid-way between Worcester, Hereford and Gloucester – hence the name which celebrates the famous annual music festival.

The vineyard is open seven days a week, except during January and February, and visitors are welcome. Wine tasting, walks, guided tours by arrangement and a retail shop are complemented by an excellent restaurant.

*OTHER PLACES
OF INTEREST*

*The Birds of Prey
Centre and Butterfly
and Natural World
Centre at Newent;
Dymock to the
north (p. 40);
Kempley to the
north-west (p. 62).*

NEWLAND

Cathedral of the Forest

All Saints Church is known, not without reason, as the Cathedral of the Forest. This lofty spacious building, with its wide nave, dates back to the thirteenth century, with each of the small chapels within it at one time having priests fulfilling different roles – teaching or taking Mass out to the miners, for example. In early days the community came together here for much more than worship. Meetings, discussions, feasts and entertainments all centred in the nave and aisles, with these public areas, at first without pews, being separated from the chancel and the altar by steps and an arch.

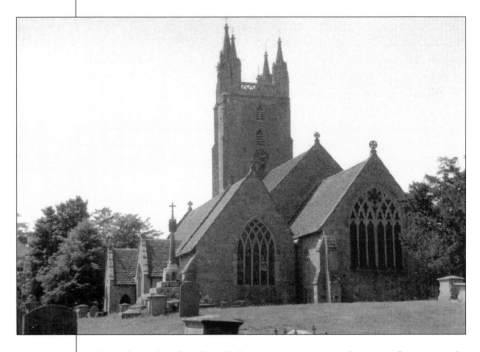

Outside in the churchyard there is a most unusual group of seventeenth-century tombs, not square and ornate as was the fashion at that time, but narrow and pipe-like. No-one seems to know why John Rannels and his family are buried like this, but the writer, at least, would very much like to find out. Facing All Saints, a neat and peaceful row of almshouses was founded by William Jones in 1615 for eight men and eight women. Jones was born in Newland but rose to become a wealthy man and a member of the Worshipful Company of Haberdashers in London.

NEWLAND

A Freeminer of Dean

The famous brass of a freeminer, of which this is a rubbing, is acknowledged as being one of the most interesting in the country. It was found set in a tomb in the medieval church at Newland, though no-one knows why. This fourteenth-century freeminer is in relief and not incised, and carries the tools of his trade (see pp. 28 and 29). The Dean Forest miners, a close-knit community, have their own ancient rights and laws from a charter dating back to the thirteenth century. Only a man over twenty-one, son of a freemining father and born within the Hundred of St Briavels, could apply to be a freeminer, and then only if he had worked for a year and a day in a mine in the same hundred. There are still about 150 freeminers in this area who have the right to dig for minerals anywhere in the forest, except beneath churchyards, gardens and orchards. The Clearwell Caves (see p. 29) used to be worked solely by freeminers.

OTHER PLACES
OF INTEREST

Coleford to the
north-east;
Clearwell to the
south-east (p. 29);
St Briavels to the
south (p. 89).

NEWNHAM ON SEVERN

The Legend of the Grasshopper and the Ant

The drawing shows a unique painted window. It can be found half-way up the carved oak staircase which faces the visitor on entering the welcoming old Victoria Hotel in Newnham. Only about 4 in square, and depicting the fable of the grasshopper and the 'aunts', it is fading now and almost impossible to read. In fact the pane is itself a copy of the original which was stolen; but a study of a transparency shows the skill of the artist. Executed nearly 400 years

ago during the Thirty Years War, when James I was king, its creator omitted much of the detail of the 'aunts', but included trees, buildings and a small figure on a horse behind the hapless giant grasshopper.

The fable reads:

> The grasshopper came unto the aunts, and
> demaunded part of theer Corne where
> upon thy did aske what hee had
> done in the sommer, and he saide
> he had song, and thy sayde
> if you song in the sommer
> then daunce in
> the winter
>
> Anno 1622.

NEWNHAM ON SEVERN

Today It Must Be Wednesday

Opposite the Victoria Hotel, St Peter's Church provides both interest and splendid views along the Severn winding below, and across to the Vale of Berkeley and the Cotswolds beyond. Most of the church building dates from 1881, following a fire, but at least six churches have been erected in this area, the first on this site in 1380, while others built lower down, were washed away by the Severn.

If you are fortunate enough to visit at 12, 3 or 6 p.m., you may enjoy listening to the carillon which plays a different tune each day of the week: 'Home Sweet Home' on Monday; 'Believe Me if All Those Endearing Young Charms' (Tuesday); 'Drink to Me Only' (Wednesday); 'The Bluebells of Scotland' (Thursday); 'Sir Philip, Lord in this Thy Mercy's Day' (Friday); 'The Last Rose of Summer' (Saturday), and *Quam Dilecta*, 'We Love the Place, O God', on Sunday. A much more original way of keeping track of the days than merely by consulting a calendar!

OTHER PLACES
OF INTEREST

Cinderford to the
north-west; Ruddle
(p. 86) and
Blakeney to the
south.

NORTH CERNEY

*Location: 9 miles
south of
Cheltenham on
A435*

MAP REFERENCE:
163: 019078

For Ease of Entry

It is unusual to see a lych-gate which swivels as this one does. It is found at the foot of the path leading to the old church at North Cerney. The name comes from the Anglo-Saxon 'lich', meaning body or corpse. In the Prayer Book of 1549 priests were requested to meet the deceased and begin the burial service here at the entrance to the churchyard. The coffin then went on into the church, and after the service was taken out again through the north door. This was the only time this door was – and still is – used. The church, rebuilt in the fifteenth century, contains a rare and complete medieval altar, here only because the heavy top was hidden in the sixteenth century and then only rediscovered in 1912. There is also a Georgian gallery, built so that it can only be reached by outside stairs.

NORTH CERNEY

To See a Manticore

On the outside wall of North Cerney's church a manticore has been incised into the stone. On the wall of the transept beneath the south window, and dating back to the sixteenth century, this creature has the head and arms of a man and the hindquarters and tail of a lion. Sadly, in the 400 years since someone painstakingly drew it, its origin and meaning have been lost.

A second drawing, probably done at the same time, is nearby on a tower buttress. It is thought this represents a leopard.

OTHER PLACES
OF INTEREST

Cirencester to the
south (p. 24);
Daglingworth to the
south-west (p. 31);
Chedworth to the
north-east.

NORTHLEACH

Location: on Fosse
Way, midway
between Cirencester
and Stow
MAP REFERENCE:
163: 113146

A Famous Family Brass

This is the upper portion of one of the many wool merchants' brasses found in the church of St Peter and St Paul at Northleach. Very worn now, it shows an early fifteenth-century group: Agnes and her two husbands, William Scors, Tailor, on the right and Thomas Fortey, Woolman. Beneath were once seen groups of her children too, but although their likenesses have gone, it is thanks to Agnes' son John, also recorded in a brass, that the church exists. The incomplete inscriptions record that William died in 1420, and tailor's scissors lie at his feet, while Thomas, a woolman and a 'renovator of roads and churches' died twenty-seven years later. The spaces in the inscriptions are ornamented with painstakingly depicted pictures of

dogs, geese, flowers, acorns, a snail, a slug, a dragon and a castle.

The church is noted for its brasses and it is unfortunate that centuries of wear mean that we can only imagine how beautiful they must have been 500 years ago.

OTHER PLACES
OF INTEREST

Keith Harding's
Museum of
Mechanical Music
and the Cotswold
Countryside
Museum in
Northleach;
Chedworth Roman
villa at Yanworth;
Bourton-on-the-
Water to the north
(p. 13).

NORTH NIBLEY

In Memory of Tyndale

Location: 2 miles
north of Wotton-
under-Edge on
B4060

MAP REFERENCE:
162: 743955

More than 300 years after his death, this monument was raised to William Tyndale, translator into English of the New Testament. Reputedly born in North Nibley in 1494, Tyndale, a humanist and a reformer, began his translation in England and continued his work in exile after meeting fellow-reformer Martin Luther. His translation was published in Europe in 1526, but denounced and suppressed in England. Smuggled copies were publicly burnt. Through the influence of Henry VIII, Tyndale was arrested at Vilvorde, near Brussels, convicted of heresy and martyred there on 6 October 1536.

His monument, rising 111 ft on a viewpoint along the Cotswold Way Walk, was designed by Teulon, an eminent Victorian architect, and built in 1866. It is signposted from the main road and the path is a long gradual climb to splendid views. Take this path which meanders upwards beneath the trees rather than the steep steps on the right – unless you have a strong heart and nimble feet! Should you wish to climb the 141 steps within the monument itself, you may, for a modest 50p, obtain a key from a house on the main road opposite the path entrance.

*OTHER PLACES
OF INTEREST*

Wotton-under-Edge
to the south; Uley to
the north-east
(p. 111); Berkeley to
the north-west (p. 6).

PAINSWICK

Spectacle Stocks

These metal stocks to the south of the church, with the yews and the tombs in the churchyard behind them, are well known and much photographed. Famous and vicious-looking as they are, the stocks date back only to 1840 and were placed here 'for the punishment of those who carry on carousels to the annoyance of neighbours'. There is said to be only one other set of 'spectacle' stocks like this in the country.

The churchyard against which any felon would rest has been called the most beautiful in England, and certainly the ninety-nine 200-year-old yews, trimmed to their neat shapes each August, are worthy of note. It is said that any hundredth tree planted fails to grow, being killed by the Devil. Here each September, the 'clypping' ceremony takes place (from Saxon 'ycleping', meaning embracing) – a service of dedication during which villagers hold hands to encircle their church.

PAINSWICK

Remember Drake

One would not expect to find a ship in a land-locked village church high in the Cotswolds and miles from the coast. But here this model stands at the back of the nave in St Mary's, a symbol of the Christian Church, and representing the believers who sail to God over the sea of life. A model of the *Bonaventure*, Drake's flagship at the Armada, and measuring about 7 ft, it was given to the church in 1971, although it is said to have been made by a local man in the 1880s.

A general history of the church, which in common with others in this area was occupied by forces in the Civil War (in this case by the Parliamentarians), may be found in interesting leaflets available at the rear of the nave.

OTHER PLACES OF INTEREST

Rococo Garden to the north; Prinknash Abbey to the north-east; Slad to the south.

Location: 1 mile
north of
Cheltenham on
B4632
MAP REFERENCE:
163: 971239

PRESTBURY

Home of a Famous Jockey

Fred Archer was a champion jockey in the late nineteenth century and this notice takes pride of place on the wall outside the King's Arms. Fred was born in Cheltenham in 1857, but came to live here two years later when his father took over the inn. He always loved horses and rode in his first public race on a donkey when he was eight! In 1873, in his final year as an apprentice jockey, he rode twenty-seven winners, and in the following year, when only sixteen, he became a champion. This title he held for the next eleven years, during which time he won 2,046 races, including five Derbys and four Oaks. In 1886 he caught typhoid fever and, tragically, while in delirium, shot himself. He was only twenty-nine and a rich as well as talented young man, for he left £60,000.

> At this Prestbury Inn lived
> FRED ARCHER the jockey
> Who trained upon toast,
> Cheltenham water & coffee
> The shoe of his pony
> hangs in the Bar
> where they drink to his prowess
> from near and from far
> But the man in the street
> passes by without knowledge
> that twas here Archer
> swallowed his earliest porridge

Directly opposite the King's Arms is a small neat thatched baker's shop, a shop made famous by its owner, Philip Delaney, who, every year, presented chocolates to the Queen Mother as she stopped on her way to the races.

*OTHER PLACES
OF INTEREST*

*Southam to the
north (p. 95);
Winchcombe to the
north-east (p. 113).*

RODBOROUGH

Home Is a Folly

On the edge of Rodborough Common, 600 ft above Stroud, and crouching now amid tall trees, stand the impregnable-seeming walls of Rodborough Fort. Known locally as 'The Folly', this sham castle was the creation of one Captain George Hawker in the early 1760s (he died about 1786). Originally called Fort George, but then known as Rodborough Fort, it was later owned by a succession of businessmen,

including Joseph Grazebrook from 1802 to 1842. In 1868 it was acquired by a Mr Halcombe, one of the last of the few folly-builders ever to have lived in Gloucestershire. Halcombe partly rebuilt it on an even grander scale. The Common on which it stands, described as 'a custom wood' in 1615, and now high open grassland, was acquired by the National Trust in 1937.

*OTHER PLACES
OF INTEREST*

*Woodchester to the
south-west;
Minchinhampton
Common to the
south; Stroud to the
north-east.*

RUDDLE

A Forgotten Port

Just south of Newnham, about 1½ miles along the A38 and down a lane which turns abruptly from the main road, lies Bullo Pill, a nearly forgotten chapter in Gloucestershire's industrial history. From this little port, between 1809 and 1928, goods were exported from Cinderford and the Forest of Dean – bark, timber and stone, but mostly coal. In its heyday, it is said that 1,000 tons of coal and stone left here every day to begin the journey along the Severn. The coal chutes have gone now, but the lock-gates remain.

The last barge (appropriately called *Finis*) left Bullo Pill in 1928 and with it the hopes of continuing export. The railway which led to it, and which opened in 1809 with the first railway tunnel in the world, under Haie Hill, has gone too. A few little boats still float above the thick grey silt, but it is difficult now to imagine the bustle and activity, and the dust and the shouting which once filled the air round this little port on the banks of the Severn.

OTHER PLACES OF INTEREST

Newnham on Severn to the north (p. 76); Cinderford to the north-west.

RUDFORD

In Memory of a Massacre

Location: 5 miles
south-east of
Newent on B4215
to Gloucester

MAP REFERENCE:
162: 778215

This obelisk at Barber's Bridge stands proudly on its own grassy bank beside a main road busy with rushing traffic, recalling a time when transport relied on people's own energy, and the horse. Then this area was just trees and grassy fields, and near here on 24 March 1643 was fought another battle in the Civil War. Lord Herbert and his Welsh soldiers were firmly entrenched at Highnam, preparing for attack from Parliamentarians Colonel Massey and Sir William Waller. After a bloody battle, Lord Herbert's Royalist army was defeated and they lay where they fell. More than 200 years later, working in that area on the excavations for the Gloucester/Hereford Canal, the late nineteenth-century workmen unearthed eighty-six skeletons. They were re-interred here and the obelisk was built with stones from Gloucester's old city walls. It records, both in English and in Welsh, that fatal battle of Highnam more than 350 years ago.

The name, Barber's Bridge, is thought to be a corruption of an earlier, more illustrative, name for the bloody battle, 'Barbarous Bridge'.

OTHER PLACES
OF INTEREST

Newent to the
north-west (p. 71);
Ashleworth and
Hartpury to the
north-east
(pp. 3, 61);
Gloucester to the
south-east (p. 51).

Location: ½ mile
south of A419, 2
miles west of Stroud
MAP REFERENCE:
162: 813043

RYEFORD

Defying Any Fire

S et beside the road to Kings Stanley, this large L-shaped building of five floors was one of the first mills to be considered fireproof when it was built in 1812. Constructed entirely of brick, its stone floors were supported not by wood, but by iron arches on cast-iron columns. Now overgrown and derelict, it sits beside sluices and waters from the Frome which provided power via five waterwheels and a beam engine.

There had been a mill here since about 1500, probably used at first for corn, but later adapted for fulling. In this area, between the sixteenth and twentieth centuries, there were several mills engaged in the manufacture of cloth. By 1853, however, this mill had reverted to corn, and subsequently became a saw mill and timber yard.

*OTHER PLACES
OF INTEREST*

*Rodborough
Common to the east
(p. 85).*

ST BRIAVELS

An Ancient Bread and Cheese Ceremony

The gatehouse to St Briavel's Castle, which has no military history and is now a youth hostel, was built in 1292–3. It is thought to have been named after a saint or a hermit who lived in the forest during the fifth century. The gatehouse is known to have been used as a prison, and graffiti on one cell wall declares, 'Robin Belcher. The Day will come that thou shalt answer for it for thou hast sworn against me. 1671'.

St Mary's Church nearby is the scene of a unique and ancient 'Bread and Cheese' ceremony. Centuries ago, parishioners paid one penny to maintain their rights to cut wood in Hudnall's Wood to the west. The money was used to buy bread and cheese and each spring, after Whit Sunday service, this was distributed, as it still is. Originally it was thrown down from the galleries to the congregation who, the *Gentleman's Magazine* noted in 1816, 'have a great scramble for them' causing 'as great a tumult and uproar as . . . a village wake'. Now the small cubes of bread and cheese are thrown from the church wall outside, and are often saved in a matchbox by their collectors, for good luck.

*OTHER PLACES
OF INTEREST*

*Clearwell and
Newland to the
north (pp. 28, 74);
Forest of Dean to the
north-east (p. 49).*

SAPPERTON

Location: 3½ miles
west of Cirencester,
south of A419 on
the Coates to
Tarlton road
MAP REFERENCE:
163: 966006

'Legging It'

Becoming overgrown now, this handsome tunnel entrance leads into a canal tunnel which, at nearly 2¼ miles long, was one of the longest ever dug in England. An ambitious project, it took five and a half years to complete, but it had no towpath. The horse was led to await the barge at the other end (which had an equally ornate portal), while the bargees moved the boat through by 'legging it' – pushing with their feet against the side or walls of the tunnel, while lying on their backs – very hard work, one would imagine. The tunnel was part of the 29-mile stretch of the Thames and Severn Canal, opened in 1789.

Paul Felix

The canal carried coal, iron ore, textiles, dairy produce and occasionally passengers in narrowboats, but with the coming of the railways its importance declined. Nevertheless, it played an important part in Gloucestershire's past until the last section between Stroud and Chalford closed in 1933.

OTHER PLACES
OF INTEREST

Chalford (p. 17)
and Stroud to the
west; Cirencester
Park to the north
(p. 25);
Daglingworth to the
north-east (p. 31).

SHAPRIDGE

Charcoal Furnace and Mill

Location: *west of*
Flaxley Woods and
1½ miles north of
Cinderford

MAP REFERENCE:
162: 674163

This sad building was once part of one of the most important charcoal blast-furnaces in England. It is thought to have belonged originally to a man called Gun who used it in the early seventeenth century as a corn mill. It was then acquired by Sir John Wintour, an ambitious Royalist who used the furnace to produce ammunition during the Civil War, swallowing up, as he did so, vast quantities of wood from the Forest nearby. It is too dangerous to explore now, but it is recorded that dates on the old iron lintels suggest it was partly rebuilt in the early 1680s. The timber ruin stands on what was once the furnace tower and beside it

can be seen the remains of a wheel-pit and a bellows room. In 1743 it became a paper mill. Its famous Royalist owner is remembered in Wintour's Leap at Broadrock, a viewpoint high above the Wye, 1½ miles upstream of Chepstow. It is said he leapt over this high cliff on his horse in 1642 while being pursued by Parliamentarians. Perhaps later, in his ironworks, he saw the opportunity for revenge.

OTHER PLACES
OF INTEREST

Littledean (see
p. 64) to the south;
Mitcheldean to the
north.

SHARPNESS

The First Commercial Nuclear Power Station

This piece of Gloucestershire's history is anything but attractive to look at. It is reached along a road west of Berkeley, a road which is, perhaps fittingly, a dead end, and it is a depressing sight – still formidable, but somehow eerie. Berkeley was the site of the world's first commercial nuclear power station. It sprang to life in 1962 when it was connected to the National Grid and in its day was a significant step forward, although it only generated about 275,000 kilowatts of power. Its life was comparatively short, for in 1988 it was closed down, and men still work on its demolition – one of them having been employed on its building. The four towers in the foreground are rusting reactors. Even in its demise, this nuclear power station is treated with respect, for those involved in its decommission have to undergo rigorous health checks as they move in and out of the building.

Beside the station are the Berkeley Laboratories, still active in nuclear research.

OTHER PLACES
OF INTEREST

Berkeley to the
south-east (p. 6);
Slimbridge to the
east.

SNOWSHILL

A Treasure Trove

Only by visiting Snowshill Manor can one appreciate the treasures it holds. Dating back to 1500, but altered over the years, the house was rescued from near-dereliction by Charles Wade in 1919. His unique collection of objects fills every room on three floors. Charles Wade (1883–1956) had a love of the past, and his enthusiasm as a collector he inherited from his grandmother. The motto on his coat of arms aptly reads 'Nequid Pereat', or 'Let Nothing Perish', and in his home (which we can now enjoy thanks to his giving it to the National Trust), we may share the myriad collection of objects which fascinated him. He bought them not 'because they were rare or valuable', but because they were 'a record of vanished handicrafts, made by the hand of a craftsman'.

SNOWSHILL

An Astrological Clock

This unusual astrological clock, with all the signs of the zodiac and more besides, is mounted on a wall in the gardens behind Snowshill Manor. It was made by Charles Wade, owner of the manor, a scholar, an architect and, as the fine lettering shows, a craftsman of some skill. Other items of his own work include a model of a Cornish fishing village now under cover in the lower garden house, and other toys and model villages in the main house itself.

Besides amassing a collection so large that it extends into the Priest's House where he actually lived, Charles Wade laid out the gardens in the early 1920s. Working to a design by Baillie Scott, he added walls, ponds and terraces, lawns and borders, so that it became the delight it still is for us to enjoy.

OTHER PLACES OF INTEREST

Broadway to the north; Hailes Abbey and Stanway to the south-west (pp. 60, 96).

SOUTHAM

Grain Distribution Point

Location: 1½ miles
north of
Cheltenham off
B4632

MAP REFERENCE:
163: 970256

I was once fascinated to read in a book on Gloucestershire that there was, in Southam's tithe barn, a 'leper chute'. As the illustration shows, there is, in fact, a stone chute protruding from the small chamber at the east end of the barn, and beside it a small window and an arched doorway atop seven steps. The barn was originally part of Pigeon House Farm, which was once monastic, and it is much more likely that the chute, although an unusual feature, was in fact used by the monks to distribute corn to the villagers and not to 'lepers'. It is thought that when alms did not take the form of grain, coins might have been passed through the narrow window. The seven-bayed timber frame barn, in private hands and currently being renovated, dates back to the late fourteenth or early fifteenth century.

OTHER PLACES
OF INTEREST

Cheltenham and
Prestbury to the
south (pp. 18, 84);
Winchcombe to the
north-east (p. 113).

STANWAY

A Cotswold Pyramid

This striking pyramid on a rise in the grounds behind the golden-stoned Jacobean manor house was erected in 1750. It was built by Robert Tracy in honour of his father John, who had died in 1735, and it commands fine views across Stanway and to the hills. Originally it was glazed, with doors and an ornate plaster ceiling. Water may be released from a pond behind the pyramid, through a culvert beneath it, and down a cascade into the canal, a flat expanse, formerly a lake, on a level with the roof of the house.

Stanway House is a family home, built between 1580 and 1640 by the Tracy family. It has only changed hands once since, other than by inheritance, and its present owner, Lord Neidpath, welcomes visitors occasionally so that we may share its history, evident in every room and in the portraits and furniture which fill them. The local tourist office will supply opening times.

STANWAY

An Ice House

The ice house is not in the formal grounds of Stanway House, nor is it mentioned in the official guide. But, although it is tucked away some distance from the main buildings, it was once an important part of life here. Like all ice houses common to great homes, it served to preserve food in the days before electricity and refrigeration. Now, however, it preserves life itself, for it has become a safe haven for bats – which is why its exact location is not revealed. There is more than enough of interest in the other readily accessible outbuildings, among them the great fourteenth-century tithe barn, the stables and the seventeenth-century gatehouse whose magnificent entrance with its scallop shell crest greets the visitor who approaches Stanway House from the main road.

OTHER PLACES
OF INTEREST

Winchcombe to the
south (p. 113);
Snowshill (p. 93);
Stow-on-the-Wold
(p. 99).

STAUNTON

Location: south of
Staunton off A4136,
along a path from
the White Horse Inn
MAP REFERENCE:
162: 542123

Ancient Standing Stones

Within a few miles of each other, and almost forming a triangle in the north-west of the county, stand three rocks, so old and so large that they have become well known just because they exist. The Suckstone (162: 542141) is the largest – here and in England. A block of quartz conglomerate, it measures 60 ft x 40 ft x 26 ft. A short distance to its south, and 900 ft above Staunton, stands the Buckstone. It was once better known as the Rocking Stone, and a Victorian engraving shows clearly why it was so called. Perfectly balanced, this conglomerate of old red sandstone rocked gently in a strong wind, until 1885 when six men took it upon themselves to push it to the ground below. Having been replaced at a cost of £500, it was concreted in place. It now looks much less impressive and rocks no more.

The Buckstone stands 12 ft high, is 13 ft wide and has an upper surface length of 20 ft. Legend says that it was used during Druidic ceremonies. The third stone, the Longstone (162: 560120) is only 7 ft high and is thought to date from the Bronze Age. It is said that it will bleed if pricked at midnight on the midsummer solstice!

OTHER PLACES
OF INTEREST

Newland (p. 74)
and Clearwell
(p. 28) to the south;
Forest of Dean
(p. 49) to the east.

STOW-ON-THE-WOLD

Corn Returns

Location: the meeting point of A429, B4068, A436

MAP REFERENCE: 163: 191257

Many don't notice this small brass box sited between windows to the left of the entrance to the Talbot Hotel. As the wording suggests, it is a reminder of a rural past, of summers before the 1700s when the Talbot acted as a corn exchange. Through this box farmers 'posted' samples of their corn to be tested for quality.

Stow, at 750 ft above sea level, the highest town in the Cotswolds, has long been a market town and stands where eight roads meet. It was once the most thriving wool market in England, and in 1724 Defoe recorded a fair where 20,000 sheep were sold. The Market Square, where the Talbot stands, is surrounded by coaching inns and old gabled houses, and is complete with stocks and a medieval market cross, which shows on its headstones Henry I granting borough status to 'Edwardstow' in 1107.

STOW-ON-THE-WOLD

More 'Wool' Tombs

S tow is not alone in Gloucestershire in having tombs which tell of the wealth merchants accumulated through wool (see Northleach, Fairford, Chipping Campden). However, these fine tombs behind St Edward's Church off the Market Square are topped by images of those important wool bales which have stood the test of time better than some of the inscriptions beneath them. Such profit from wool had earlier made possible the rebuilding of the Norman church here, and through the centuries St Edward's has been maintained and added to. Now the visitor is made welcome in eight languages as he enters the porch, although doubtless at the end of the Civil War some visitors were not so welcome. At that time, the church was used to imprison Sir Jacob Astley and some of the 1,500 Royalist troops captured by Parliamentarians at the battle of Stow (1646). A memorial to Captain Francis Keyt, who died then, is in the chancel. Those interested in church art and architecture will find the notes available in the church of value.

OTHER PLACES OF INTEREST

Lower Swell to the west (p. 68); Bourton, the Slaughters and Wyck Rissington to the south (pp. 13, 66, 118).

SUDELEY

A Noble Castle and Home

Location: ½ mile
south of
Winchcombe off
B4632

MAP REFERENCE:
163: 032276

Sudeley Castle's history stretches back over 1,000 years, and its connections with the Crown are obvious to the visitor who wanders round its magnificent rooms. Built in 1469 by Ralph Boteler, it figured largely in the life of Richard III who built the Banqueting Hall, and of the royal Tudors – Henry VIII and Anne Boleyn stayed here in 1532; Elizabeth I came three times; it became the palace of Queen Katherine Parr when, as Henry's widow, she came here on her marriage to Sir Thomas Seymour, and here she is buried. Later it became the headquarters for Prince Rupert

during the Civil War, but suffered much damage at the hands of Cromwell's troops. Then in 1830 it was bought by the Dent family of Worcestershire, famous for their gloves, who employed Sir Gilbert Scott to restore it to its present magnificence. So much history, so many references to the famous through the centuries, and still a family home.

Lord and Lady Ashcombe welcome visitors to the house and gardens between April and October and the castle also hosts special events throughout the summer.

SUDELEY

'A Court for Owls'

Owls and barns traditionally go together, but it is an unexpected pleasure to come across this charming group tucked away in the ruins of the tithe barn at Sudeley Castle. They were recently commissioned by Lady Ashcombe and sculpted by Mr Douglas Barrett. He used as his models a group of barn owls which he had sketched while living in Scotland, but they could just as easily have been modelled on the many owls which must have lived in this barn throughout the centuries. It is to be hoped that this family will never 'fly away', for it is a delight to discover them, dozing amid old-fashioned roses and climbing plants in the ruins of their barn.

OTHER PLACES
OF INTEREST

Winchcombe to the north (p.113); Cheltenham and Prestbury to the south-west (pp. 18, 84).

SYDE

Syde's 'Hidden Gem'

Location: 7 miles
south of
Cheltenham and
west of A417

MAP REFERENCE:
163: 950109

This tiny church, crouching at the foot of wide steps beneath the trees, is hidden away, a peaceful fragment of 'rural England', and yet it is only ¾ mile from a busy modern highway.

Syde is one of the smallest and oldest parishes in England, and St Mary's Church, mainly fourteenth century and called 'a gem' by one writer, is a microcosm of ecclesiastical history. Here, passing through a Norman entrance, one finds Charles II's coat of arms, a votive cross and a roundel touched by pilgrims in the Middle Ages, tiny eighteenth-century box pews (seating in all not more than sixty), a floor at a level higher than it was

before the Reformation, and 'modern' gas lighting. Since 1600 only just over fifty marriages have been solemnized here.

The adjacent building is a fourteenth-century tithe barn, a warehouse for Cirencester and Gloucester Abbeys for tithes of corn and hay, root crops, fleeces and timber, with the priest's house at the lower end of the barn.

OTHER PLACES
OF INTEREST

Crickley Hill
Country Park to the
north; Elkstone to
the north-east
(p. 43);
Daglingworth
(p. 31) and
Misarden Park
gardens to the south.

TEDDINGTON

*Location: 5 miles
east of Tewkesbury,
at the crossing of
A435 and A438*
MAP REFERENCE:
150: 339964

'*Strange Travellers the Way to Show*'

It is perhaps fitting that this old finger-post, pointing in five directions, should be situated at Teddington Hands. Since it is at a meeting of five ways, is this how Teddington got its unusual name? Now sited on the green beside an inn which uses its picture as a symbol, it is safe from modern traffic, traffic which its original seventeenth-century donor could never have visualized. Worn, almost indecipherable letters in the stonework, remember 'Edmund Attwood of the Vine Tree' who erected the post 'strange travellers the way to show'. An Edmund Attwood lived in Teddington at the beginning of the 1600s, and later generations of his family, it is believed, maintained the post. It is very rare to find a surviving finger-post nowadays.

*OTHER PLACES
OF INTEREST*

*Tewkesbury to the
west (p. 108);
Tredington to the
south (p. 110).*

TETBURY

A Wool Centre

Tetbury was established as an important market town and wool centre as early as the thirteenth century. By 1622 wool and yarn sold here was said to be 'inferior to none in England' and in 1655 the Market House was built. Originally gabled, it soon became used for the wool trade alone, and all that formerly sold in the streets was brought here for weighing and selling. In 1740 it was re-roofed and extended to allow for more storage space and a larger room above, then used for courts. It was extensively remodelled in 1817 when the gables were removed from the roof. The house still serves as a weekly market-place, the upper oak-beamed room being used as a meeting hall. It is also the centre for the Woolsack Races held each May, when relay teams race up and down Tetbury's steep streets carrying fifty-pound woolsacks.

Beside the house, the Chipping Steps, medieval and cobbled, were for centuries the site for Mop Fairs.

TETBURY

An Early Gothic Revival Church

The illustration shows why Tetbury's Church of St Mary is said to have the fourth highest tower in England. Reaching a height of 186 ft, the tower and its spire were rebuilt from the ground in 1891. Prior to that the church had been rebuilt between 1776 and 1781, and was one of the earliest Gothic Revival churches in the country. Designed by Francis Hiorn of Warwick, its spacious and theatrical interior is unusual in having high box pews, some of which can only be entered via ambulatories on either side of the church. The whole is lit by its original eighteenth-century brass chandeliers, each carrying thirty-six lights. One of the instigators of the rebuilding was Samuel Saunders, who lived at The Grove in Tetbury Upton. In the church we learn nothing more of him, except that:

> In a vault underneath
> lie several of the Saunderses
> late of this parish; particulars
> the Last Day will disclose.

TETBURY

Our Own Beer

This building on Hampton Street leading into Tetbury was the site of a brewery established, as it clearly notes, in 1800. It was begun by a John Cook who took over a former wool warehouse built by one Matthew Bamford. For years Cook ran a successful business, even though two other breweries were begun in 1820 by John Warn and Thomas Witchell. These separate breweries continued until the early twentieth century when Warn took over Witchell's. At about the same time, 1913, Cook was absorbed by the Stroud Brewery Company. In the 1930s, in common with many others in the country who were fighting competition from large businesses, both Tetbury's breweries closed.

OTHER PLACES
OF INTEREST

Tetbury Police
Bygones Museum in
Long Street;
Chavenage to the
north (Elizabethan
manor house);
Westonbirt
Arboretum to the
south-west.

TEWKESBURY

Truly Belonging to the People

Tewkesbury Abbey is not a cathedral, as its appearance might suggest, but a parish church. Consecrated in 1121, the present building was founded on the site of an eighth-century monastery. The tower, the largest Norman tower in Europe, is 46 ft square, rising to a height of 148 ft at the top of its late seventeenth-century pinnacles. But for the foresight of the people of Tewkesbury, this beautiful building might not exist. At the Dissolution, when it was to have been destroyed, they raised money to buy it – even by sixteenth-century standards, a bargain, one feels, at £453. Inside there is much of interest, including a modern memorial stone to Victoria Woodhull Martin (1838–1927). An American and a freethinker, branded by puritans in her own country for her views on sex and women's suffrage, she was the only woman to stand for the American presidency. In later life she lived in Worcestershire and became a much-respected pillar of society, noted for her philanthropy.

TEWKESBURY

Home of the Baptist Faith

In a small court near the abbey, and almost opposite the John Moore Countryside Museum, is a narrow alleyway. Here still stands an early Baptist Chapel, one of the oldest in England, whose records date from 1655 (the first English Baptist congregation was formed about 1608). Behind the neat and restored black and white exterior, the rooms are equally neat and austere, white walls beneath heavy wooden beams, with forms, the furniture of that period, round the walls.

OTHER PLACES
OF INTEREST

The Inns in
Tewkesbury;
Deerhurst to the
south (p. 32);
Tredington to the
south (p. 110).

TREDINGTON

Back to the Jurassic Age

One cannot go further back into Gloucestershire's past than to a fossil like this of an ichthyosaur, a fish lizard which lived over 150 million years ago. Unexpectedly, it can be found, just discernible, embedded in the floor of a church porch at Tredington. Fortunately it lies to the right, against the wall, so that people have been able to avoid walking on it, and it has not become too damaged. This particular fossil is about 9 ft long, although these marine reptiles could grow to 36 ft in length.

St John's Church itself is unusual in having a wooden tower atop its Norman style stonework. This had been a feature since Elizabethan times, although the present tower was rebuilt in 1883. The cross noted on Ordnance Survey maps is an ancient one with a 9 ft shaft formed from a single stone.

OTHER PLACES OF INTEREST

Tewkesbury (p. 108); Deerhurst to the west (p. 32); Gloucester to the south (p. 51).

ULEY

Hetty Peglar's Tump

*Location: 1 mile
north of Uley,
beside B4066*

**MAP REFERENCE:
162: 790000**

This long barrow (below), a smooth undulating green hump, is clearly visible from the road, and a five-minute walk along a well-worn path at the edge of a field brings one to the entrance (right). It is difficult to appreciate that this prehistoric burial ground, 40 x 30 yd wide and 10 ft high, was probably built 3,000 years BC. On excavations in 1821 and 1854 it was found to consist of a stone-built central passage 20 ft long running from east to west, with a chamber at the end and another on either side. The entrance was formed by two upright stones topped by another 8 ft long. It is said that two stone axes and thirty skeletons were found within it. The barrow's more popular name derives from the fact that the land on which it stands was owned in the seventeenth century by a Mistress Hetty Peglar.

*OTHER PLACES
OF INTEREST*

*Owlpen Manor just
north at Uley;
Nailsworth to the
east; Nibley to the
south-west (p. 81).*

WESTBURY ON SEVERN

The Watch Tower

This solid tower, with its slender shingled spire, looms over its church a short distance away. The tower, once a garrison watch tower, built in 1270, was originally attached to a wooden church which was burnt down. At the same time as this was replaced in the early fourteenth century, about 30 yd away, the 160 ft spire was added to the tower. Collectors of data might be interested to know that when it was reshingled in 1937, 60,000 shingles and 100,000 copper nails were used. It is said that, solid as it appears, it has been known to shake when the bells are rung, even though it has been strengthened.

The church holds a chained book, not a bible, but a copy of Foxe's *Book of Martyrs*. It mentions the only Forest martyr to die for his beliefs. James Baynham, son of the lord of the manor, was burned at the stake at Smithfield on 30 April 1532.

*OTHER PLACES
OF INTEREST*

*Westbury Court
Gardens (National
Trust), next to the
church; Newnham
on Severn to the
south (p. 76);
Littledean (p. 64)
and Cinderford to
the west.*

WINCHCOMBE

Seven Legs?

Location: 7 miles
north-east of
Cheltenham on
B4632

MAP REFERENCE:
150: 023282

There is much to see in Winchcombe and these stocks may, at a casual glance, seem like any others still preserved. They stand outside the town hall, itself built in 1853 and now housing the Tourist Information Centre beside the Folk and Police Museums. But look closely, and you will see that they are different. It is said that the seventh hole was reserved for the use of a one-legged member of the community who often found himself on the wrong side of the law. True story or not, these stocks must be unique.

WINCHCOMBE

Find the Imp

Visitors to the beautiful medieval church of St Peter are generally well aware of forty grotesque gargoyles which decorate the exterior, but many miss the Winchcombe Imp inside. He, too, is medieval and was cleverly carved on the oak screen which, although originally placed between the chancel and the nave, now stands at the west end of the nave. One can imagine the carver smiling as he worked, little imagining, perhaps, that his imp would make others smile, too, more than five hundred years later.

For those who cannot spot him, the imp is in the second circle from the left in the photograph.

WINCHCOMBE

Safely Locked Away

Other things of interest in St Peter's Church include this alms box in the north aisle. Made of oak, it was carved, somewhat roughly, in the sixteenth century and has three locks. This design was the result of a decree made by Edward VI in 1547, which stated that such boxes should have three locks – the minister holding one key and two churchwardens holding each of the others. It would seem that no-one was trusted in those days.

Further along the north wall, in the chancel, kneels the sad figure of Thomas Williams of Corndean who died in 1636. Opposite him is an empty recess where, it is said, he hoped the figure of his widow would finally be placed. But he waits in vain, for she married again and left express wishes that she should be buried with her second husband.

There are many more interesting things which are pointed out in excellent guidebooks within the church.

WINCHCOMBE

Treasures for the Steam Enthusiast

A short walk along Gloucester Street from the church brings one to what appears to be a fairly ordinary house. But Mr Petchey's back garden, which to the uninitiated may look a jumble, is in fact a Mecca for the railway enthusiast. Here, for a little while, he may imagine or remember being a railwayman, pulling levers, changing signals, ringing bells or clipping tickets. Crammed into this half-acre is memorabilia from the great days of the railways – tracks, signals, notices (about 500), ledgers, uniforms, china, silverware, all the things which Mr Petchey, a train-spotter from his schooldays, 'didn't like to see being lost'. So his first acquisition, a Midlands Railway restriction notice dated 1875, has grown over the years into this fascinating 'hands-on' museum. And while would-be station masters reminisce or exchange information, the ladies may admire Mrs Petchey's herb garden. Set far from the house, it is a re-creation of a medieval garden with its medicinal and culinary herbs. Here, too, children may play in safety or enjoy the ducks and rabbits which are part of the family.

WINCHCOMBE

Trainee Sign Writer?

Mr Petchey's railway collection includes this odd sign, rescued from Coleford in the Forest of Dean. It was an 1880s gradient marker for the Severn and Wye Railway. This must have been a new challenge for the signwriter, for the whole thing is almost a mirror image. Not only are the Ns wrong, but the 30 and 60 should be interchanged.

The museum is generally open in the afternoon from Easter to October, but check before visiting.

OTHER PLACES OF INTEREST

Winchcombe Pottery, Becketts Lane; Hailes Abbey and Stanway to the north (pp. 60, 96); Sudeley Castle to the south (p. 101); Gloucestershire–Warwickshire Railway at Toddington.

WYCK RISSINGTON

Location: down a
minor road 2 miles
south of Stow off
A429
MAP REFERENCE:
163: 191215

A Mosaic Maze

Even without the light reflected on this mosaic on the wall inside St Lawrence's Church, it is quite difficult to follow the correct path through the maze. Canon Harry Cheales, rector here from 1947 to 1980, had a dream which led him to construct a maze in the rectory garden, first of boulders and then of high hedges. He completed it in 1950. It represented the fifteen Mysteries of the Gospel – five joyful, five sorrowful and five glorious – with sins and temptations in each 'dead end'. Each year on the feast of St Lawrence, 10 August, he led his parishioners through the maze, passing each Mystery in the correct order without the procession crossing itself. The Mysteries were indicated by signs, and opposite the fourteenth, representing the falling asleep of the Blessed Virgin, was a sign, LIFE AFTER DEATH, inviting those who did not believe to turn back. The path continued through a dark tunnel, representing Death, and on to a flower-filled Paradise in the centre. The mosaic was created as a memorial to Canon Cheales after his death in 1984, by John Bayliss, as the original maze had been destroyed.

OTHER PLACES
OF INTEREST

The Slaughters to
the north-west
(p. 66); Stow-on-
the-Wold to the
north (p. 99);
Bourton-on-the-
Water to the south-
west (p. 13).

ACKNOWLEDGEMENTS

I should like to offer thanks to all those who have been so generous in their help: to Lord Neidpath and Lord Bathurst, the Sudeley Estate and Douglas Barrett, Mr and Mrs J.E. Turner, Maureen Townley, Mr Jonathan Wright, Mr Chapman of Newent, Derek Pearce and Dr Tomlinson, Mr and Mrs Petchey of Winchcombe, Elizabeth Henson, Mr larks, Mr Maler-Wright, Charles Clark, Jack Farley, Paul Felix, Roger Parrott, Brian Clarke, Rupert Harding, David Viner at the Corinium Museum, the Gloucester Folk Museum, the Gloucester Records Office and the Cheltenham Tourism Centre among others; and last, but not least, Lucy and Jonathan.

BIBLIOGRAPHY

Victoria History of Gloucestershire
Childs, M. *Discovering Churchyards*
Davis, C.T. *The Monumental Brasses of Gloucestershire*
Jones, B. *Follies and Grottoes*
Mee, A. *The King's England – Gloucestershire*
Ottewell, G. *Gloucestershire Countryside*
Phelps, H. *The Forest of Dean*
Stanier, P. *Shire County Guide – Gloucestershire*
Verey, D. *Gloucestershire and the Cotswolds*
Verey, D. *Vale and Forest*
Withers, C.J.W. *The Cotswolds*